**My Girl**
and
**Frozen Assets**

'In **My Girl** . . . Keeffe movin[g]
gnaw into people's lives, und[ ]
happiness. He draws his characters with such sympathy and deta[il]
that the audience finds itself entirely absorbed by their story . . .
the dialogue has a violent energy and salty frankness . . . with
scenes of great tenderness and observant comedy.'
Charles Spencer, *Daily Telegraph*

'a fine and touching account of married poverty in a rented flat in
Leytonstone . . . the marital relationship is beautifully dissected in
the present misery . . the play is a little gem.'
Michael Coveney, *Financial Times*

'**Frozen Assets** . . . contains sustained stretches of flashingly
truthful dialogue and splendidly imagined comic scenes.'
Irving Wardle, *The Times*

**BARRIE KEEFFE** was born in East London in 1945. His plays
include **Only a Game** (Shaw Theatre, 1973), **Scribes** (Greenwich
Theatre, 1976), **A Mad World, My Masters** (for Joint Stock, 1977),
**Frozen Assets** (RSC, 1978), **Bastard Angel** (RSC, 1980), **Better
Times** (Theatre Royal, Stratford, East London, 1985), **King of
England** (Theatre Royal, Stratford East, 1988) and, for the
National Youth Theatre of Great Britain, **A Sight of Glory** (1975),
**Here Comes the Sun** (1976), and **Up the Truncheon** (1977). For
the Soho Poly Theatre Club he has written **Sus** (1979; also seen at
the Royal Court) and two trilogies: **Gimme Shelter** (**Gem, Gotcha,
Getaway**) also staged at the Royal Court in 1977, and **Barbarians**
(**Killing Time, Abide With Me, In the City**) which played
Greenwich in 1977. His work for TV includes **Nipper, Hanging
Around, Waterloo Sunset**, adaptations of **Gotcha, Gem,** (retitled
**Not Quite Cricket**), **Abide With Me** (retitled **Champions**) and a
serial, **No Excuses** (published in novel form) based on his play,
**Bastard Angel**. Keeffe was Thames TV Playwrights' Award resident
dramatist at the Shaw Theatre in 1977 and writer in residence
with the RSC in 1978. In 1979 **Gotcha** received the French theatre
critics' Prix Revelation, and his radio play **Heaven Scent** won a
Giles Cooper Award. For the cinema he wrote the screenplay for
**The Long Good Friday** (1981), for which, in 1983, he won the
Mystery Writers of America Edgar Allen Poe Award.

**Methuen's New Theatrescripts** series offers frontline intelligence of the most original and exciting work from the fringe.

# My Girl

# Frozen Assets

*Two Plays by*

*Barrie Keeffe*

**Methuen Drama**

**A Methuen New Theatrescript**

**Frozen Assets** *first published in 1978 by Eyre Methuen.*
**My Girl** *first published with* **Frozen Assets** *as a paperback original in Great Britain in 1989 by Methuen Drama, Michelin House, 81 Fulham Road, London SW3 6RB and distributed in the United States of America by HEB Inc, 70 Court Street, Portsmouth, New Hampshire 03801.*

*A CIP catalogue record for this book is available from The British Library*

*ISBN 0-413-62200-2*

Printed and bound in Great Britain by
Cox & Wyman Ltd, Reading

*The front cover photograph is of Meera Syal and Karl Howman who played* Anita *and* Sam *in the Theatre Royal, Stratford East production of* **My Girl**. *(Photo © Nobby Clark)*

# Introduction

There's an eleven year gap between these two plays. I think the link between them is that **Frozen Assets** was written before Thatcher and **My Girl** after ten years of her. Both are set in East London – both are about people I know, in places I know. **Frozen Assets** began when I walked into my flat in East London and met a Borstal boy turning it over: he was on the run. We had a couple of beers and he left and I started writing the play. It ends optimistically. **My Girl** was billed 'A Love Story' when the Theatre Royal, Stratford East produced it. It's about hanging on to keep your love alive without money. It's ten years after Thatcher. It doesn't end optimistically.

Over the years, and in different countries, I've made changes to **Frozen Assets**, updating it. I think now it's a period piece and so I haven't indicated the changes in this volume.

I met the Buddy of **Frozen Assets** again when he came to see **My Girl** at the Theatre Royal. He's happily married now, has three children – all girls – and doesn't steal cars anymore. But when he met the character that Sam in **My Girl** is based on, he offered to get him one at a vastly reduced cost. Ten years after Thatcher . . .

Barrie Keeffe, London, 1989

# My Girl

*for Philip Hedley*

**My Girl** was first performed at the Theatre Royal, Stratford East on 6 March 1989 with the following cast:

**Sam**       Karl Howman

**Anita**     Meera Syal

*Director*  Philip Hedley and Barrie Keeffe
*Designer*  Jenny Tiramani
*Lighting*  Stephen Watson

The setting throughout is **Sam** and **Anita**'s furnished flat in Leytonstone, East London. February and very cold.
The action takes place in one month.


**Music**

Before Scene One: Ronnettes *Baby I Love You*
After Scene One: Eddie Floyd *Knock on Wood*
Before Scene Two: Introduction to film *The Blues Brothers*
After Scene Two: Otis Redding *Try A Little Tenderness*
During Scene Four: Ronnettes  *Baby I Love You*
After Scene Four: Otis Redding  *My Girl*

# Act One

Scene One

*Music before play: Ronnettes* Baby I Love You

*A furnished flat in Leytonstone. Big, ugly old furniture – we can see at once the furnishings* **Sam** *and* **Anita** *have added – totally different style and so much nicer. Especially the table lamp with the Tiffany shade.*

*Once lights up on the empty room, sound of a baby crying above the sound of Mahler on Radio 3.*

**Sam** *(bellowing from the kitchen)* If that baby doesn't stop that –

*Baby screams louder from bedroom and* **Sam** *shouts louder from kitchen as radio music continues.*

I said, if that baby doesn't stop that bloody –

*Even louder baby screams.* **Sam** *bursts in wearing pants, socks and anorak, a pair of rose pruners in one hand.*

Anita! Anita! Anita!

**Anita** *calmly comes out of bedroom. She is heavily pregnant and moves slowly.*

Your bleeding kid is calling you!

**Anita** Did you say something?

**Sam** I said: your bleeding kid –

**Anita** *(very calmly)* *Our* kid.

**Sam** I disowned her when she started that racket at half past six this morning –

**Anita** She's teething –

**Anita** *begins to collect and fold nappies hanging to dry over fireguard in front of electric fire.*

**Sam** Not for much longer – I've got the rose pruners.

*He snaps them.*

I shall rip her troublesome teeth out. One at a time. Every one of them. Put her out of her misery and us out of ours.

**Anita** You would.

**Sam**  Too bloody right, I *will.*

**Anita**  (*ever so calm*)  Sam, it's the cold that irritates her. It's freezing in that bedroom. So cold. Even you admit that. The condensation on the window is still ice even when this room's warmed up. I've lighted the oil heater in there now. So she'll be all right, when she gets warmed up.

**Sam**  Cost of paraffin.

**Anita**  Once she's warm, she'll drop off.

**Sam**  And when might that be?

*He sips from mug of tea.*

**Anita**  When her teeth stop hurting.

**Sam**  Better be soon . . . or honest . . . I might bloody smother her. With a foam pillow. Every time I look at her she cries.

**Anita**  (*matter of fact*)  You never wanted her. She knows. Instinctively. That she's unwanted by her father.

**Sam**  Where did you pick up that crap? You've been reading Claire Rayner again.

**Anita**  *turns off radio.*

**Anita**  Turn this off . . . it might help.

**Sam**  Wish we could turn *her* off like that.

**Anita**  I bet you do.

**Sam**  Sure I do. Saturday I'm gonna soundproof that room. Go down to Do It All and buy a great big box of them polystyrene tiles, with holes in them to absorb the noise and I shall spread lashings of superglue all over them and hammer them all over the walls and . . . silence will reign supreme.

**Anita**  You dozy sod. We'll not hear her them.

**Sam**  That is precisely the point. It's . . . it's the acoustics in this place. Fantastic –

**Anita**  High ceilings –

**Sam**  My point. If it was bigger Bruce Springsteen could rehearse his band in here. Clarence blowing in the lav . . . them move in here –

**Anita**  And us move out? I'd like that.

**Sam** I'd like that.

**Anita** Then why don't we do something about it?

**Sam** Anita, I'm doing everything humanly possible about it. I am working all the hours God sends to get something done about it.

**Anita** *picks baby toys from floor, holding her back, every movement painful.*

**Anita** I should have married that bloke in Squeeze.

**Sam** Ha.

**Anita** He was mad about me.

**Sam** So you said he said.

**Anita** *He* said. He had the pick of the groupies after Jooles Holland. He said I was the only virgin he took out three times.

**Sam** He said.

**Anita** He did.

**Sam** *looks down out of window.*

**Sam** Oh here's the paper boy – late again!

**Anita** Told you, phone the newsagent up and complain –

**Sam** Leave off. You know how *many* Mister Patel's there are in the phone directory –

**Anita** Sssh. Hear it?

*Pause. They both listen. Silence.*

**Sam** What?

**Anita** She's stopped.

**Anita** *creeps to ajar bedroom door to listen.*

**Anita** You can just hear her breathing . . .

**Sam** Yes. I tell you, I've never heard a baby cry as loud as Katey.

**Anita** Don't be daft.

*She packs away clothes.* **Sam** *now begins to get dressed.*

**Sam** Really, I haven't, I tell you. Other people's babies gurgle and howl and vomit and shit in a kind of sweet, endearing way. They're pink and blotchy and soft and smooth and make you want to kiss their arses. But her –

**Anita**  Her? Who's *her*?

**Sam**  Kate!

**Anita**  So you *do* remember her name then?

**Sam**  What you going on about? 'Course I remember her bleeding name.

**Anita**  Her, her, her. Kate's her name!

**Sam**  Wednesday's child is full of woe
And daddy's gonna drown her in her pissy po.

*Off, sound of papers falling through letter box.* **Sam** *goes to get them.*
**Anita** *leans on ironing board, dabbing her eyes with cuff of the baggy
cardigan. She composes herself as* **Sam** *re-enters room. He's reading sports
page of* Guardian.

**Sam**  Bloody hell, Orient won at Colchester last night. Two nil.
If they win every remaining match and no other team in the
fourth division . . . plays . . . they could just avoid relegation.

*He trails off. Realises* **Anita** *is crying into cardigan sleeve.*

Hey Anita . . . Anita . . .

*She waves him away.*

Hey, please . . . don't get upset.

**Anita**  Upset, he says. How am I supposed to feel?

**Sam**  I know, I know love.

**Anita**  But you *don't* know. You only have her –

**Sam**  Kate –

**Anita**  Kate! A couple of hours a day but –

**Sam**  But you have her –

**Anita**  I have her all the time.

**Sam**  You do.

**Anita**  And it's not fair. All the time, every day, day after day . . .
and in the night when she wakes up. All the time I have to cope
with her on me own . . . and I can hardly walk now.

*She clasps her bulging belly.*

I look like a . . . steamroller.

**Sam** *laughs, hugs her, kisses her.*

**Sam**  No you don't, you clown.

**Anita**  Yes, I do! You said it! When I was lugging the big shop upstairs, you said I took so long, a steamroller could have done a three point turn in a cul-de-sac faster.

**Sam**  I didn't mean it.

**Anita**  That's what you said.

**Sam**  Just a little joke. To make you grin. To see your smile. When you smile, hot dog sellers all over London burst into song! Give us your smile, Princess.

**Anita**  Don't call me Neets!

**Sam**  I didn't, I didn't.

**Anita**  I hate you calling me Neets.

**Sam**  I called you Princess.

**Anita**  That's beside the point. I don't care what you call me. You're mad, barmy. Why should I care what you call me? You've only been out of bed ten minutes and already you've threatened to pull out your daughter's teeth – my daughter's! And drown her in the piss pot and –

**Sam**  *Kate's* piss pot!

**Anita**  And suffocate Kate in a soundproof room.

**Sam**  But when I said those things . . . I meant them in a sweet, endearing, affectionate way.

**Anita**  You're holding a pair of rose pruners in your hand.

**Sam**  Ah. Couldn't find the pliers. Trying to fix the Ascot in the kitchen – it's buggered again.

**Anita**  I know it is.

**Sam**  You should have told me – warned me.

**Anita**  I told you last night.

**Sam**  I forgot. You did.

**Anita**  I've been telling you for weeks it's been on the blink. Yesterday it nearly blew me eyebrows off. We've got to get it properly mended for once and for all.

**Sam**  But I've already mended it properly.

**Anita**  Sam, you can't mend Ascots with sellotape and Blu Tac

**Sam**  I did me best.

**Anita**  I know you did, darling but . . . unless we call in the experts to do it properly, there'll be a catastrophe. The whole street will blow up. And then where will we be?

**Sam**  As soon as I get to work, I'll ring them – who?

**Anita**  The Gas Board.

**Sam**  I'll ring the Gas Board.

**Anita**  They take forever. Unless you tell them you can smell gas.

**Sam**  I'll tell them I can smell gas and since I'm a chain smoker on doctor's orders . . . it's a fucking emergency.

**Anita**  You have to make an appointment, even for emergencies.

**Sam**  Then I'll make an appointment. I'll tell them I'm expecting to smell gas and the emergency will reach devastation proportions next Tuesday at half past ten . . . Greenwich Mean Time.

**Anita**  'Half past ten in the morning or evening, Sir?'

*They laugh. She sniffs, blows nose.*

**Anita**  Let's have a ciggie, Sam. Go on. Just one.

**Sam**  Give it another fifteen minutes . . . only a quarter of an hour to wait.

**Anita**  I'll have one now and not another . . . till I've done the ironing.

*He thinks, then rolls a cigarette and gives it to her. She inhales luxuriously.*

**Anita**  I definitely won't have another one till . . . Woman's Hour. Oh Sam, it's that north wind that does it. It's so bitter. The drafts coming in through the window in the bedroom –

**Sam**  I'll fix them on Saturday. Properly.

**Anita**  'Cause them rolled up newspapers just don't work. The leaks –

**Sam**  Use a different newspaper – *Guardian*. So many leaks. Leaks. Geddit?

**Anita**  Oh yerrs. Very droll.

**Sam**  Drafts, probably the drafts keep making Katey cry. Surprised she ain't crying icicles instead of tears.

**Anita**  Yesterday afternoon, on Woman's Hour – they said the Ice Age is going to start again.

**Sam**  Yeah, in our bedroom. Soon there'll be polar bears in the back yard turning cartwheels.

**Anita**  Will it affect Spain?

**Sam** *has been stuffing reports into his battered briefcase. He stares at* **Anita**.

**Sam**  I beg your pardon?

**Anita**  What I mean is – it'll be so nice to have one really decent holiday in Malaga or somewhere before it starts freezing over in Spain.

**Sam**  We'll have one.

**Anita**  Oh good. 'Cause the Ice Age'll really mess up the tourist trade in Spain, won't it? I suppose they'll have to take up winter sports instead. Ski-ing and that.

**Sam**  Oh yeah, definitely.

**Anita**  On Woman's Hour, they said when the Ice Age comes, only the fittest will survive.

**Sam**  We'll be all right, Anita. Straight after the birth we'll get down to some serious training. Canadian Airman's exercises on Hackney Marshes every Sunday morning –

**Anita**  Sam, they were being serious! It's already starting. The whole of the Northern Hemisphere will be affected. – We'll all have to go and live in Australia and South Africa and the South Pole.

**Sam**  For gawd's sake, Anita. Not next year. Another thousand years before they have the winter Olympics and Eddie the Eagle in the Sahara. Thousands of years.

**Anita**  Really? Well, they shouldn't say things like that on Woman's Hour – especially not when they've got pregnant women listening. They make it so worrying. They always have something for us to worry about. If it's not about destroying the ozone layer – I haven't used an aerosol since they said about everyone could die of sunstroke through the hole in the ozone layer –

**Sam** Take it easy –

**Anita** What I want to know is: if the aerosols destroy the ozone layer, why won't the sun come through the hole so strong it'll melt the Ice Age?

**Sam** Bloody good question.

**Anita** What'll happen?

**Sam** The Ice Age'll melt and we'll all drown. Only kidding. You worry too much Anita.

**Anita** I've got a nervous disposition.

**Sam** You'll be all right. You've got a lucky face. You and Katey and Cyril here (*Touches her bulge.*) and me – we'll all be all right. Got a feeling.

**Anita** Yeah. We're survivors.

**Sam** We are.

**Anita** Would you like some porridge? Or an egg? Proper breakfast –

**Sam** Let's skip the egg – toast is all right.

**Anita** Egg, egg! Sorry, the last thing I want you die of is semolina poisoning. Always hated it at school dinners. But I didn't know semolina could kill you.

*She looks at him.*

Got it wrong . . .

**Sam** Salmonella.

**Anita** Salmonella! I know the difference . . . just me concentration at the moment . . . muddle up the words . . . makes me sound so stupid . . .

**Sam** You're not stupid. (*He hugs her again.*) Lick away your tears, wash them away – taste the salt.

**Anita** It's mascara you can taste.

**Sam** Wash away the salty taste of your mascara with me furry tongue.

**Anita** Didn't remove it last night. Always put it on for you Sam . . . lot of women don't bother, they give up and don't bother looking nice for their man when they're this far gone. I like to look nice for you when you come home.

**Sam** You do.

**Anita** I'd do me hair and all, if the Carmen rollers were working.

**Sam** Must be a broken wire. I'll fix them on Saturday –

**Anita** You do notice that I've put on make up, and look nice for you . . . when you get home from work?

**Sam** Yeah, I notice.

*Pours himself another half mug of tea.*

Important thing though is . . . doing your exercises every day.

**Anita** Yeah.

**Sam** Taking your Fefol pills?

**Anita** Yeah.

**Sam** No anti-bodies in your rhesus negative?

**Anita** Not a sniff of one.

**Sam** And you're at the clinic again this afternoon?

**Anita** Me mum's coming round to collect me at half past one. It might be the last time there, before he arrives.

**Sam** Yeah . . .

**Anita** Next Thursday . . . I've got such a feeling . . . I'm so sure that's when –

**Sam** He might be early.

**Anita** You can never sure when. I know. Just like waiting for the buses – just when you've given up hope the 128'll turn up, lo and behold two of them do. Know what I mean?

**Sam** Bet you know more things that I'll ever know.

*Pause.*

Don't forget what Mrs Jackson downstairs said . . . just hammer on the floor with the rolling pin and she'll phone up the midwife and –

**Anita** What if the pain's so bad I can't get to the kitchen to get the rolling pin?

**Sam** Use your initiative.

**Anita** I'll do that.

*She laughs, kisses him. She's been deliberately worrying him.*

I was only winding you up. Everything's under control, husband.

**Sam** Anita we ain't gonna stay here much longer. That's a promise. We will get out of this doss house. A tacky furnished flat, shared bathroom – that a man in my position should be in this position is a total enigma to me.

**Anita** See, what worries me Sam is . . . with another kid, there just won't be room for us here. This was lovely when it was just the two of us, even with Katey but . . . four of us . . . no security and –

**Sam** Anita –

**Anita** What I mean is –

**Sam** I know.

**Anita** After three years, at least I thought the council –

**Sam** These last three years, it's amazing the council can even afford to employ social workers –

**Anita** I just mean . . . when you became one . . . now three years later. I didn't think things would still be the same . . .

*Pause.*

You know what I mean?

*She looks away. He gathers last file and glances at it before putting it in his briefcase.*

**Sam** I should have written up this referral last week.

**Anita** I read the one about the Bengali girl – it was ever so sad –

**Sam** Don't read this one. It's ripe porno.

**Anita** How do you mean?

**Sam** Six-year-old kid. Teacher found she kept masturbating in the classroom –

**Anita** Really?

**Sam** How the bloody hell should I know? Advanced sexual awareness, the teacher reckoned. Of course, after all the Cleveland shite. How can you tell? Father seemed all right when we checked him out. But how can you be sure? What's a child molester look like? What's a pervert look like? What's a *Sun* reader look like?

**Anita** What did Adolph Hitler look like? I mean . . . I know what you mean. How do you know?

**Sam** I'm so scared Anita . . . that every day I'm making mistakes . . . the wrong decisions . . .

**Anita** That's because you've got too much work on now . . . you're working too hard.

**Sam** So they prosecuted the dad, he took the rap and we got the kid out of care . . . most perfect mother and child, emotional reunion . . . and a week later, call from the hospital, kid beaten up again, this time even worse. Been the mother all the time. We missed it. Lucky to be alive . . . Christ.

**Anita** Wasn't your fault Sam.

**Sam** Went to see the doctor yesterday, Anita.

**Anita** Did you? Why?

**Sam** Don't know . . . sort of ill feeling.

**Anita** *pauses at ironing she's begun.*

**Anita** What did the doctor say?

**Sam** He told me to piss in a bottle and keep taking the pills.

*Pause.*

**Anita** What sort of bottle?

**Sam** A?

**Anita** Pills? I meant – what sort of pills?

**Sam** I dunno. Any old junk. Whatever he prescribed. He was unconcerned, sort of detached. He kept yawning.

**Anita** He's very considerate to me.

**Sam** Yeah, but you're different. You have something discernibly wrong with you, visible symptoms. You've got a bun in your oven. Sorry, I didn't mean that . . . Anita, what I'm trying to say is . . . He was so bored with me in front of him. Yeah, I could understand that . . . outside his waiting room full . . . asthmatics wheezing and gobbing on the worn out carpet and coughing and dribbling and incontinents pissing and farting on the orange plastic chairs and ga-ga geriatrics sucking cough candies and Vic chest rub steaming up from their woollen long johns and reading *Woman's Own* upside down and kids who'd got their heads stuck in steering wheels nicking car radios and policemen with champagne corks stuck up their arseholes and everywhere snotty hankies and blocked up sinuses and . . . poor old doc must be as disgusted with people's physical decay as I've been by . . . their social sickness. No immunisation for this job.

*He shakes his head.* **Anita** *attentive. He's very serious.*

Three years at the centre . . . tramping round in other people's miseries . . . Ought to kit us out with lobotomies . . .

**Anita**  Sam –

**Sam**  Not trained to deal with this, Anita. This sort of poverty, this sort of desperation –

**Anita**  What did the doctor say?

**Sam**  He didn't even look at me. Just said: 'So what's wrong with you this time Mister Casey?' *He* asked *me* what was wrong. I said, 'How come doc that you know I'm Mister Casey? You haven't looked at me.' He said: 'I recognise your voice Mister Casey.' I said: 'For all you know I might be an imposter using my voice as well as my name.' He looked at me and said, 'All right, what's the matter, what are your symptoms?' I told him. I said I was a social worker. I said I was feeling rather depressed and helpless and powerless. He said when did I start feeling like this? I said since last April when Mrs Thatcher changed the benefits system. I said I felt I was drowning in air. He wrote me a prescription. I tore it up in front of him. And left. Anita, we're going to have to change GP's.

**Anita** *clasps his hand.*

**Anita**  Sam, you can't keep changing doctors every time one can't find something wrong with you. There's nothing physically wrong with you –

**Sam**  I'm not all right – what about all these boils I keep getting?

**Anita**  I know –

**Sam**  There must be a reason –

**Anita**  Not ill. Run down, yeah. Very tired, overworked, depressed and . . . your age Sam. In three weeks time you're going to be 30.

**Sam**  Oh holy Jesus.

**Anita**  But Sam, that's not old.

**Sam**  It's not young though, is it?

**Anita**  Old people think you're young. Mister Trishingham said –

**Sam**  Old Bert Trishingham, bless his urine stained jock strap, is still peering through his telescope in the attic looking for Napoleon's invading army. Still gloating over Mafeking and wondering why the selectors dropped W.G. Grace.

**Anita**  Compared to him you're young.

**Sam**  Once I hit 30 – then never again shall I be described as a young man.

**Anita**  But Sam –

**Sam**  Talking to a bloke from the *Recorder* the other day – was asking him why grammatical competence was considered a handicap in local journalism . . . he said an interesting thing. House style, they call it. They write: 'A young man appeared in Newham magistrates court today', if he's 29 or under. From now I'll be: 'A *man* appeared in court this week.' Thirty years, racing on. Ascots exploding, wallpaper peeling, Carmen rollers breaking down . . . volcanic eruptions of yellow boil pus on the bed-sheets . . . (*Points.*) That settee's only eight-years-old and its arms are threadbare. I'm surprised my fucking arms haven't fallen off by now.

**Anita**  (*laughing*)  Oh Sam, you do make me laugh. You're such a dozy prat.

**Sam**  Thank you. Seems I just get over that Monday morning feeling and it's Friday afternoon. I'm months behind on writing up me reports. Hopeless. Days drifting into weeks, and nothing getting better, nothing being achieved. Referrals piling up. Can't do anything for anyone anymore. Now we can't even get grants for essentials. Clever woman, that Thatcher – now it's loans. How can the fucking poor afford to pay back a loan for a cooker, for a new bed . . . for essentials? This bloke the council sends round. Can't do anything to help them. Just a nosey parker asking questions . . . and . . . and . . . getting worse for us, Anita. Thought of a mortgage, instead of getting closer . . . just drifting farther away. Nothing getting better . . . no passionate affairs with exotic women – over cocktails at the Zanzibar.

**Anita** Oi.

**Sam** You should have married that bloke with the Squeeze.

**Anita** I only went out with him three times.

**Sam** Someone's being chucking tomatoes at it again.

**Anita** What's that?

**Sam** Someone's been chucking tomatoes at our VW again.

**Anita** They probably think its been abandoned.

**Sam** Don't it strike you as a bit odd, though. Third time someone's splattered the car with tomatoes . . .

**Anita** Oh yeah, so it is. Funny that.

**Sam** Like an omen.

**Anita** Mmm.

**Sam** Bloody peculiar thing to do.

**Anita** Yeah.

**Sam** Three times.

**Anita** *absent mindedly flicking through magazine delivered with* Guardian.

**Sam** If I was of a superstitious nature –

**Anita** Right –

**Sam** Right, right –

**Anita** Pardon?

**Sam** Nothing interesting . . .

**Anita** This is interesting, Sam. It's the Year of the Snake.

**Sam** You what?

**Anita** This year, the Chinese horoscope . . . listen Sam, this is amazing . . . 'After the eventful year of the dragon . . .'

**Sam** Oh fuck.

*He secretly lights another cigarette as* **Anita** *continues to read from the magazine.*

**Anita**  'The year of the Snake offers a time of reflection, re-adjustment and a time of considerable opportunity. It will be very much a year when hard work, enterprise and dedication will be rewarded –'

**Sam**  Ha!

**Anita**  ' – right across the whole spectrum of human activity and considerable advances will be made. This is especially likely in the fields of arts, energy conservation, medicine and social change. It was the Year of the Snake when the Russian Revolution began.'

**Sam**  That's gotta explain the tomato vandalism.

**Anita**  There might be something in it, Sam . . . me brother was born in the Age of Aquarius.

**Sam**  That wasn't the Chinese horoscope.

**Anita**  I never did understand what Age of Aquarius meant –

**Sam**  I think it was a sort of Hampstead equivalent of Nice One Cyril.

**Anita**  Have you got everything? I could do some sandwiches, for your lunch.

**Sam**  Thanks all the same. Raining again. I wish that bloody car would start. I'll have a look at the starting plugs on Saturday. Get it going again.

**Anita**  It'd be handy if you did. In case you had to dash me to the hospital . . .

**Sam**  Even the bloody muggers know this is a no-go area . . . and can't leave a perfectly respectable hundred and fifty quid VW unattended without having it plastered with rotten fruit . . . no wonder we never have any visitors here.

**Anita**  Why don't you do something about it, Sam?

*He hesitates. She is very serious and calm.*

**Anita**  Get a decent life –

**Sam**  I'm a qualified social worker. Three years at university. Got an MA in social work – can't get more decent than that!

**Anita**  But you don't get a decent wage. Well, at least a job with accommodation. Anything instead of this tatty, rented flat.

**Sam**  On the pittance I get – not exactly in a position to hit the mortgage stakes.

**Anita**  When will we ever be?

**Sam**  Chin up, Dunkirk spirit Anita. If I play my cards right . . . survive another couple of years in Newham – that's providing Thatcher still has social services in a couple of years, that – I don't get murdered by one of me cases, don't get beaten up too often when I can't get them a cooker . . . if I get promoted to team leader, become an administrator . . . instead of doing the job I trained to do, wanted to do . . work me way up through the bureaucracy . . . could be earning enough to get a mortgage by the time Katey's having her 'coming out ball'. If I haven't gone mad . . . hang up me cycle clips and work behind a desk in The Grove. No danger then of getting knocked off me bike by a swaggering convoy of travelling families on the Beckton By-Pass. Just catch up with the realities of these times – switch off caring.

**Anita**  You upset me when you talk like that, Sam –

**Sam**  I have to keep biting me lip to stop telling me cases about our financial situation. In a bed and breakfast place at Bayswater the other day – seeing a referral, poor family . . . I was so tempted to nick a bacon sandwich. Only the thought of being plastered over the front page of the *Recorder* brought me to my senses.

**Anita**  They'd probably have spelt your name wrong anyway.

*They both laugh.*

**Sam**  Don't worry, something'll work out. Got a lucky feeling. Year of the Snake and all that.

**Sam** *makes fresh mug of tea in kitchen.* **Anita** *removes letter she sees protruding from pocket of* **Sam**'s *coat on sofa. She opens it as* **Sam** *watches, appalled.*

**Anita**  It's a letter from our bank manager.

**Sam**  If I get any more of his letters, people are going to start talking about him and me.

**Anita**  He says there've been other letters, correspondence.

**Sam**  I seem to recall the exchange of one or two missives.

**Anita**  I didn't see any of them.

**Sam**  I didn't want to bog you down with the complicated machinations of our fiscal manoeuvrings.

**Anita**  A?

**Sam**  All right, I admit when it comes to fulfilling my responsibilities as the family breadwinner, I'm an out and out chauvinist.

**Anita**  (*reading letter*)  'Dear Mister and Mrs O'Casey –'

**Sam**  See, can't even get my name right, the moron. It must be a pre-requiste for the job – banking. You always add an O.

**Anita**  'Thank you for your letters of the 18th, 21st and 24th. I'm gratified to learn that you look upon me as a father figure.'

**Anita** *stares at* **Sam**.

'And I'm touched to read that you intend to dedicate your book of poems to me.'

*She stares at him again.* **Sam** *makes vague hand movements.*

**Anita**  'But am I to understand that your slim volume of verse is the sole means by which you intend to repay your unauthorised overdraft which at close of business yesterday stood at 376 pounds and 71 pence. I look forward to your reply as soon as possible. Yes, you may call me Charles in the dedication for the book.'

*Her hands shake as she glares at the letter.*

Nearly four hundred fucking quid!

**Sam**  He's got it wrong. I'll challenge that figure. Even if I have to go to the Court of Human Rights in Brussels.

**Anita**  Jesus Christ! Where's all the fucking money gone Casey?

**Sam**  Inflation . . . increased interest rates . . . the Big Bang . . . the City crash, donations to the Armenian earthquake appeal –

**Anita**  Where's four hundred quid we never had gone?

**Sam**  Calm down, Anita –

**Anita**  I haven't even got a cheque book.

**Sam**  That eliminates one possibility.

**Anita**  Jesus, nearly a month's wages in debt.

**Sam**  He's got it wrong, and I shall prove it.

**Anita**  I haven't spent it. You've spent it. What on? Why? When? And what the fuck is this . . . slim volume of verse?

**Sam**  I can explain that –

**Anita**  You've gone barmy, round the bend –

**Sam**  Just a technical hitch in the bank's computer –

**Anita**  'Very touched that you're proposing to dedicate your book of poems to me.' You're touched all right. Mad and bad and –

**Sam**  Dangerous to know.

**Anita**  What?

**Sam**  Mad, bad and dangerous to know – that's what they said about Byron.

**Anita**  Who?

**Sam**  Lord Byron. He wrote books of poetry.

*He ducks as she hurls cushion at him.*

**Anita**  What's it supposed to mean, this letter? What you wrote to him – God, Sam. Book of poetry. You only ever send joke birthday cards to me, not even a verse in them.

**Sam**  A pragmatic deception necessitated by fiscal mal-occurrence –

**Anita**  You what?

**Sam**  Whopper of a fucking lie. Anita, don't keep bashing me head in. I don't know where the money's gone. But since we have run an 'unauthorised overdraft' that size, and he had the decency to mention it to me before he started bouncing cheques all over the place –

**Anita**  'Touched that you look upon me as a father figure.' 'Yes, you may call me Charles in the dedication.'

*She begins to cry.*

**Sam**  For Christ's sake, not that again, Anita. You've already howled twice this morning. This rate we'll both start bleeding shrinking.

*She sobs wailingly.*

**Anita**  Where'd all the money go Sam?

**Sam**  Most of it went on buying the car, right!

**Anita**  Car, car? You mean that bloody heap of rusting junk out there?

**Sam**  Investment. Council scheme for buying a car. Low interest rate, I jumped the gun. Got in fast so as not to miss the bargain –

**Anita**  But it don't go.

**Sam**  It did when I drove it home after buying it. That's when it stopped working. When I got it here. Bloody funny that –

**Anita**  So why have you spent our money, if they said they'd lend you the money for it, take a couple of quid a week out of your wages?

**Sam**  Yeah, but first they assess it. The deal. Inspect the car. And when they inspected it the council thought it was a right pile of shit and wouldn't give me the fucking loan. Bastards.

**Anita**  But why didn't you wait till they'd assessed it before you gave over good money for it?

**Sam**  Because, because – I would have lost out on a bargain. I wish Charles here (*Taps letter.*) had bounced *that* bloody cheque.

*She's too choked up to speak.*

I'll get it patched up, working again, through it's MOT. Then flog it. Probably make a profit on it, we will. It's a bargain. It would be if it worked.

**Anita**  Sam, you're hopeless.

**Sam**  Can't be good at everything.

**Anita**  Just one thing'd do. Oh Sam, you're not worried?

**Sam**  Nar, course not. We'll sort something out. At least there's a salary coming in. Respectable profession. Bank manager ain't gonna shaft someone like me, man in my position.

**Anita**  I worry. Another baby coming – all that expense.

**Sam**  Yeah well, know what they say. Keep it for 14 days and if you don't like it, send it back and choose something else from the catalogue.

*She laughs.*

**Anita**  What I mean is, this should be a happy time for me.

**Sam**  It is . . . in a way.

**Anita**  It should be summer and I should be sunbathing in a garden, on a hammock . . . roses everywhere. Like a wonderful country garden . . .

**Sam**  Got it, got it – got the point. Sorry.

**Anita**  Hammock stretched out between lovely trees in blossom. Laying there reading *Vogue* and choosing baby clothes and you bringing me soft ripe peaches and Turkish delight and wearing a beautiful Laura Ashley maternity dress. *Me*, I mean – not you!

**Sam**  I know, princess.

**Anita**  Us not moving round like Romanies every other year, one set of furnished rooms to another. It's dangerous here, Sam. I worry.

**Sam**  I know you do.

**Anita**  Can't leave Katey out the front in her pram to get a bit of fresh air in the summer in case she gets stolen.

*Pause.*

I thought things'd get better, not worse.

**Sam**  There's hundreds worse off than us.

*Pause.*

**Anita**  Sam – I get ever so frightened.

*Pause. She holds her bulging belly.* **Sam** *stamps on floor.*

**Anita**  It's not that, Sam. No, not yet. A pain, yes. But not labour pains.

**Sam** (*shouts down to the floor*)  I'm sorry Mrs Jackson – it's a false alarm!

**Anita**  Just a sort of empty pain.

**Sam**  How do you mean?

**Anita**  I mean . . . all them years you were at university, gave up your job to train, get the qualifications to be a social worker . . . hard up those years yeah, but . . . looking forward to the day you qualified and . . . what I mean is, I didn't think all these years later, it'd be this bad. With a family, and us like this. No carpets on the stairs, and sharing a toilet with other tenants and . . . ovens you can't get clean no matter how hard I try and scrub it and believe me the grime just won't come off whatever I use to –

**Sam**  All right, all right – hey, I believe you.

**Anita**  And sharing the bath with other people. The man down the corridor who works at the kebab shop, when the lavatory's blocked up I've seen him – he widdles in the bath.

**Sam**  Dirty fucker. How do you know?

**Anita**  I saw him doing it when he'd forgotten to lock the door.

**Sam**  Well, I tell you – if I catch him, I'll amputate his prick with the rose pruners and turn it into shish kebab. With red hot chilly sauce stuffed down the hole.

*They both laugh. He kisses her tenderly. He checks his watch.*

**Anita**  Sorry me moaning, didn't mean to.

**Sam**  I reckon you're entitled to now and again.

**Anita**  Just now and again?

**Sam**  Only every now and again, mind.

**Anita**  Just sometimes I feel frightened that things aren't going to improve – just get worse.

**Sam**  Won't. That's a promise. I've got a lucky feeling. Well, better get going – off into the infinite cosmos.

**Anita**  Sam, just one more?

*He rolls another cigarette.*

**Anita**  After the birth, stop smoking – never again.

**Sam**  It's a mug's game.

**Anita**  See, coming out of Tescos yesterday, Sam – great crowd of people . . . and there was this tramp hanging around outside. You know, like they do. And he kept staring at me at the bus stop – really staring. And then blow me down, if he don't come right up to me – and he asks me for money.

**Sam**  What did he say?

**Anita**  He said: 'Madam' – yeah I thought that was odd.

**Sam**  Madam?

**Anita**  Yeah, he said: 'Madam – spare the price of a cup of tea.'

**Sam** How much did you give him?

**Anita** A quid. He didn't go up and ask no-one else, just me, Why? Why me?

**Sam** I dunno. You've got a loving, sympathetic face.

**Anita** It's not the first time it's happened, Sam. It's happened before. At the station, Liverpool. Street – when I worked in the city. It happened four or five times at Liverpool Street. And it happened at Brighton once. If I was invited to a garden party at Buckingham Palace, bet your bottom dollar some bloody smelly tramp would come up to me and ask me for money.

*She shakes her head, very serious now.*

I keep thinking, them sort of down and outs can see something in me when they look at me. In my eyes. They always look right into my eyes. They know. You and me, people like us – they can see we're going to end up as helpless as them.

**Sam** Come off it. Three Snowballs and you're anyone's.

**Anita** I'm being serious, Sam. I'm being serious. I don't mean a wino. I have nightmares sometimes, about if everything goes wrong. We can't pay our bills. If everything goes wrong. Wheeling Kate and Cyril in a pram down Leyton High Road . . . with a couple of carrier bags and all our clothes piled on the pram and cooking pots and saucepans tied on and banging about . . . all our worldly belongings on the pram . . . and I just kept walking and walking . . . I can't help it. It scares me Sam.

**Sam** Just, that at the moment . . . we're batting on a dodgy wicket, Anita. Keep a straight bat.

**Anita** Yes.

**Sam** Watch out for the googlies.

**Anita** That's the least we can do Sam.

**Sam** Keep our eye on the ball.

**Anita** Then bash the bastards for six!

**Sam** Now you're talking. That's the spirit. We'll be all right. Just you wait and see. These sort of worries – one day we'll look back on them and laugh. (*Sings from Springsteen's* Rosalita.) 'One day we'll look back on this and it will all seem . . .'

**Anita** '. . . funny.'

*He scratches under his arm, gasps.*

**Anita**  What's the matter?

**Sam**  Just an itch under me arm. Okay though.

**Anita**  Sorry holding you up. You'll be late for work.

**Sam**  That's okay. I've got to go straight onto a call. She's always late getting up so –

**Anita**  Who is? She?

**Sam**  Girl, single mother. Got to tell her that her daughter, baby girl, she's going into care. A bit tricky this one.

**Anita**  Going into care for good?

**Sam**  Until she's able to cope. She's a bit down, a bit volatile . . .

**Anita**  How old's the baby?

**Sam**  Eight months. Lovely kid.

**Anita**  But why?

**Sam**  The mother, she's only eighteen herself. Kept neglecting the kid. Just couldn't cope with the baby. For everyone's good, neighbours complained and . . . police broke into the flat. Found the baby on its own, crawling across the floor to the electric fire . .

**Anita**  O God, the bitch. I just don't understand that Sam. I just can't help hating a mother who does that to –

**Sam**  The mother's a kid herself. Spite for the baby she did't want, maybe. Depriving her of her youth . . . I dunno. Something like that. Some fucking reason. But this morning I've got to tell her her kid's been taken into car.

**Anita**  Will she mind?

**Sam**  She's a mother. It's her baby.

**Anita**  But will she mind?

**Sam**  Now she's gone, she'll want it back like mad.

**Anita**  Will she be allowed to have her back?

**Sam**  Not for a while.

**Anita**  Poor baby.

**Sam**  Poor mother.

*He stares out of window.*

**Sam** Bleeding car.

**Anita** I could ask me brother today . . . cause he's good at mechanical things . . . if he could have a look at it, the plugs and that . . . try and get it started.

**Sam** If you see him today, well, yeah. It's a very simple job. It shouldn't be beyond him. I was going to do it myself on Saturday anyway.

**Anita** I'll ask him.

**Sam** Do that.

**Anita** After the hospital, I'm going round the shops with me mum anyway. So I'll ask him. Me mum and me, we're going to look for your birthday present.

**Sam** Oh, great. But, don't go crazy. Nothing too expensive in view of the letter from the bank manager, know what I mean –

**Anita** Sam, don't fret. I've been saving a bit every week from the housekeeping. You'll like what I'm going to get you. I know exactly what to get.

**Sam** Well –

**Anita** See you later then.

**Sam** Yeah.

**Anita** When you get home.

**Sam** Don't know what time that might be. A couple of evening visits tonight.

**Anita** See you when I see you then.

*She kisses him as he turns to leave. Off, baby begins to cry. Blackout and music: Eddie Floyd's* Knock on Wood.

## Scene Two

*Loud music. Instrumental overture from film* The Blues Brothers. *Lights up. Morning in the living room of the flat. Weak sunshine through the windows as* **Anita** *bounds in from bedroom dancing – as much as she can – wearing black trilby hat and black sunglasses. She wears fur coat* *inside out for the warmth and mimes to the record playing.* **Sam** *is sleeping on sofa under blanket – and is disturbed by her impromptu cabaret. She seems very happy. She uses broad American accent.*

**Anita**  Good evening ladies and gentlemen, and welcome to the Universal Amphitheatre. Well, here it is, the late nineteen seventies going on nineteen eighty five.

*Blast of horn section on record. Now we realise she's impersonating John Belushi.*

You know, so much of the music we hear today is pre-programmed electronic disco. We never get the chance to hear the master blues bands practising their craft anymore.

*Increased tempo. She dances about.*

By the year two thousand and six, the music known as the blues will exist only in the classic records department of your local public library. So tonight, ladies and gentlemen, while we still can, let us welcome from Rock Island Illinois the Blues Brothers Band of Joliette, Jake and Elwood Blues . . . The Blues Brothers!

*Climax of brass section.* **Sam** *leaps from sofa on which he's sleeping.* **Anita** *is trying to get him to dance.*

**Sam**  You gone barmy – what the fuck? Christ Anita. I was asleep. What's the matter with you?

**Anita**  Happy, ain't I?

**Sam**  I thought you'd gone bleeding mad.

**Anita**  The Blues Brothers movie. John Belushi and –

**Sam**  Yeah, yeah. All of that –

**Anita**  It always makes you laugh. (*She mimes Belushi.*) We've got a hundred and sixty miles to go to Chicago. We got a half pack of cigarettes and a full tank of gas, it's dark.

**Anita**⎫
**Sam** ⎬  And we're wearing sunglasses.

**Sam**  Where did you get this?

*He tries on her trilby hat. She puts sunglasses on him.*

**Anita**  This brilliant shop in Greenwich. It does all period clothes. My brother took me there, he was getting something to wear for a Blues Brothers party tonight . . . and the bloke in the shop, Welsh bloke . . .

really nice . . . I made him laugh doing me impressions of the film and . . . so he gave me the hat and the glasses, for nothing.

**Sam**  He probably thought you were John Belushi, fat sod.

**Anita**  Don't joke, Sam. John Belushi's dead. Cocaine killed him. He spent about three thousand pounds a week on it. The man in the shop in Greenwich told me. And then he died.

**Sam**  Let that be a lesson to us Anita. Let us vow here and now never to spend three thousand pounds a week on cocaine.

*He groans and holds his head.*

**Anita**  Hangover?

**Sam**  Nar, nar. Just not as vivacious as you are. What about Katey?

**Anita**  Me mum's got her today.

**Sam**  Oh yeah, that's right –

**Anita**  (*hugs him*)  So just you and me. The whole of Saturday together. My favourite day – you and me –

**Sam**  Yeah. (*Pulling away from her.*)

**Anita**  What's the matter. You look terrible . . .

**Sam**  I feel like I've just hitch-hiked across the Sahara.

**Anita**  Here's some tea.

*She sets down mug of tea beside him.*

**Sam**  Ta. Thanks a lot.

**Anita**  Anything I can get you?

**Sam**  This is fine.

**Anita**  Look like you need something. What would you like?

**Sam**  What would I like? I'd like to be put asleep for about a week. I'd like to be comatose and pumped full of vitamins. And have electrodes attached to all me muscles to tune me up to Olympic Games standard while I sleep. So when I wake up – I'd wake up a new man. On the National Health. That's what I'd like.

**Anita**  How's your new boil?

*He moves his arm cautiously.*

**Sam**  It's in fighting form this morning. What's the time?

**Anita** Half past ten –

**Sam** Feels like half past ten boil angst. Yerrs, definitely a bit of the half past ten irritation here.

**Anita** The water'll still be hot in the kettle. I'll bathe it and change the dressing.

**Sam** Yeah. That'll be nice. Bloody nasty thing.

**Anita** Good job you've still got some ointment left over from the last one.

**Sam** But used up all the antibiotics. Why do I keep getting all these boils? There must be a reason I *keep* getting them.

**Anita** Perhaps it's another omen?

**Sam** The doctor said it was only to be expected at my age. Crap. Said blokes my age are prone to them. Bollocks. So I said to him: 'What you're saying is, like – I see a geezer in the street, face smothered with pussy lumps like misty craters of the moon – I just go up to him and say: Boils. Boils. Happy thirtieth birthday!

**Anita** *laughs.*

Christ, it's cold.

**Anita** At least it's not raining.

**Sam** My, my – you are a perky little thing this morning. Bloody freezing in here.

**Anita** Draft coming in through the window frame in there –

**Sam** I'll fix that on Saturday.

**Anita** It *is* Saturday.

**Sam** My bloody arm. I can hardly move it.

**Anita** Didn't play you up last night though, did it?

**Sam** How do you mean?

**Anita** Time you got back last night . . . I never heard you come in.

**Sam** You was fast asleep when I got in.

**Anita** I usually hear you.

**Sam** Yeah, well – last night I was later than usual.

**Anita** What time did you get in?

**Sam** I dunno . . .

**Anita** Roughly?

**Sam** After midnight, I suppose.

**Anita** After midnight? You didn't come into bed when you got in.

**Sam** I didn't want to disturb you and Katey . . . so I crashed out in here.

**Anita** Second night this week you've slept in here . . . on the settee.

**Sam** What do you mean? I'm not keeping a record, I'm not making notes of –

**Anita** I just happened to notice it's the second time this week, that's all I said –

**Sam** Then let me consult me fucking Filofax.

*He dips in jeans pocket and pulls out a stack of screwed up pieces of paper – they scatter like confetti.*

Sorry. Disorganised Filofax. Don't seem after all to have kept notes on how many times I've –

**Anita** Sam, all I meant is – I just wondered why the last couple of nights you've slept in here, instead of with me.

**Sam** Well, quite frankly . . . at the moment, size you are . . . not exactly an abundance of space in the bed for the both of us.

*Pause.*

**Anita** That's true. Sorry . . . anyway, not for much longer.

**Sam** No. Can't be.

*He moves arm.*

Oh Christ, this really is hurting . . .

**Anita** I'll put the water on the boil again . . . bathe it for you.

**Sam** Ta, Anita. Steam it a bit, put on a fresh dressing . . . make it feel a lot better.

*As he sips mug of tea,* **Anita** *goes to doorway of kitchen. Pauses.*

**Anita** Sam . . .

*Pause.*

Um, Sam . . . everything's all right with us, isn't it?

*Pause.*

You and me. Everything *is* all right with us, isn't it?

**Sam** Yeah, yeah. Of course it is. What do you mean?

**Anita** You sleeping in here the last couple of nights . . .

**Sam** I told you. So we can both have a good night's sleep.

**Anita** I know that's what you said but –

**Sam** But what?

*She shrugs.*

**Anita** I miss waking up in the morning, opening me eyes and you being there. That's what I miss. You're not fed up with me, are you?

**Sam** Don't be daft.

**Anita** Good. You're not unhappy are you?

**Sam** Unhappy?

**Anita** Are you?

**Sam** Anita, I'm living the life of a total hedonist – without all the hassle and hard work that would be necessary to actually enjoy meself.

**Anita** What? Oh Sam, I don't know what you're talking about half the time.

**Sam** Sorry love. It's the bloody words that get in the way and muddle you up, don't they.

**Anita** Don't be nasty to me!

**Sam** I'm not being *nasty* to you!

**Anita** You are being nasty.

**Sam** I am not.

**Anita** Something's the matter with you!

**Sam** It's the fucking boil . . . hurting.

**Anita** Honestly, Sam? Is that all?

**Sam** It's driving me nuts. That's all . . . just putting me in a bad mood, that's all it is . . .

**Anita** *relieved, smiles. Goes into kitchen.* **Sam** *pulls off T-shirt, then tugs off elastoplast under his arm pit. Groans.* **Anita** *returns with steaming bowl of* *water, carrying cotton wool, lint and ointment. Sits beside him on sofa to treat the underarm boil.*

**Sam** Bleeding hairs . . . (*This as he gasps, pulling off last attachment of elastoplast.*)

**Anita** Don't know why we have to have hairs under our arms.

**Sam** Suck up the sweat.

**Anita** I wonder if birds sweat under their wings? When they're flying, I mean.

**Sam** Good question. One day we'll buy a parrot. Teach it to talk. And when it's learned how to talk, we'll ask it.

*She places hot-water-soaked lint on boil. Then clasps towel under his armpit to hold in the heat.*

**Anita** Say if it hurts.

**Sam** *groans, then shakes his head. She repeats this procedure through following dialogue several times then finally re-dresses the boil with ointment and new plaster.*

**Anita** I think the reason you keep getting these boils Sam . . . is that you're ever so run down.

**Sam** Run down implies some sort of actual momentum . . . I think I've sort of stopped moving altogether. A strange lethargy.

**Anita** You need a rest.

**Sam** I need something.

**Anita** You need a holiday. A week off – get away from it all.

**Sam** I've put in for a week – when Cyril's born.

**Anita** I mean a proper week off. They owe you a week.

**Sam** You know that's out of the question. We're still two short –

**Anita** If you don't have some time off sometime you're going to get really ill.

**Sam** I will have time off. A few days when Cyril . . .

**Anita** What I think would be nice –

**Sam** When you come out of hospital with Cyril –

**Anita** What I was thinking would be nice would be . . . having a little holiday after Cyril's born and . . . if me brother gets the car working,

and me mum looks after Katey and Cyril, you and me to have a drive
out to Suffolk and maybe stay with –

**Sam**  Not all this again, Anita. What's brought all this on again –

**Anita**  All I'm saying is –

**Sam**  You've talked on the phone again to Jane and Ronnie haven't
you?

**Anita**  Yes, as a matter of fact I have.

**Sam**  I knew it.

**Anita**  Why do you get so mad? Anyone'd think you're jealous of
Ronnie, just because he's bettered himself –

**Sam**  Bettered himself, what do you mean – bettered himself?

**Anita**  Bettered himself, that's what he's done.

**Sam**  Sold out, that's what he's done.

**Anita**  You're jealous.

**Sam**  Jealous!

**Anita**  Because he's improved himself. Lovely big old house in
Diss with fields and a pond and countryside all around and –

**Sam**  They're running an old people's home! Looking after barmy
old people.

**Anita**  Jane said it's beautiful out there. A million times better than
Newham. No stress, no violence, no –

**Sam**  Running an old people's home in the shires? I always knew
Ronnie was less than ideologically sound, always suspected there
was an entrepreneurial aspect to his character –

**Anita**  They've got a nice house. A house for babies to grow up in.
And they're happy.

**Sam**  He's sold out.

**Anita**  What they've got is better than this.

**Sam**  Anywhere's better than this.

**Anita**  Jane asked if we'd like to go down to the country for a long
weekend . . . stay with them and have a look at –

**Sam**  No fucking way. I don't want to help him run an old people's
home. I don't want to give up and leave here and be run out into

the wilds of . . . the countryside.

**Anita**  Why not?

**Sam**  Because it would be giving up.

**Anita**  Give me a proper reason.

**Sam**  It's a matter of pride.

**Anita**  I don't understand you.

**Sam**  What's new about that?

**Anita**  We're living here like paupers . . . and you say no to a decent place and say it's because of pride.

**Sam**  Anita . . . I'm not going to get moved out of London just because we're . . .

*Pause.*

**Anita**  Because we're what?

**Sam**  Poor.

**Anita**  Very poor

**Sam**  A lot better off than the really poor.

**Anita**  People who laugh at you . . . you admit it, they laugh at you for trying to help them, and you say it yourself – you can't help them. So what's the fucking point staying here?

*Pause.*

Read that report last night . . . family put in that lovely house on the Isle of Dogs . . . fancy putting a homeless family in a place like that.

**Sam**  Cheaper than a bed and breakfast in Bayswater –

**Anita**  Bloke who owns it –

**Sam**  Left it vacant. Investment.

**Anita**  Porsche outside the house one side next door –

**Sam**  Roller the house the other side, I know.

**Anita**  You put down in the report, you didn't know what to say to him.

**Sam**  I didn't.

**Anita**  Sam, how poor is poor?

**Sam** Poor is . . . the inability to buy 16 goods and services generally accepted as the basic necessities of life. Like beds, for everyone in the family, a warm, waterproof coat, mats in the living room, some kind of meat or fish to eat three times a week. That's poor.

**Anita** We're poor then . . .

**Sam** Yeah, we're poor.

**Anita** And there'll be four of us soon.

**Sam** Bloody kids.

**Anita** That's a wicked thing to say.

**Sam** Sometimes I feel wicked.

**Anita** You mustn't feel like that!

**Sam** Don't be so bloody naive. When you can't sleep at night, when you lay awake in the early hours listening to Bert Trishingham coughing his old guts out and wondering if it's rats you can hear scratching under the floorboards . . . be honest, don't you think how different our lives would be if it was just you and me, just the two of us? You earning, two salaries . . . no kids. See Harry coming into the centre, his missus working . . . holidays in Spain, suntans . . . his fucking suede jacket. Bloody 30 soon and I've never been able to afford a suede jacket. It's insanity.

**Anita** I wanted Katey. And I want Cyril here. I want children. It's natural.

**Sam** Is it? I think those kind of emotions are going decidedly out of fashion in these modern times, darling.

**Anita** You wanted to be a father.

**Sam** I wanted . . . the idea of it. Fucking you to have a baby. Instead of just for sex. I liked the idea of that at the time. That's all I am sure of. I don't feel grown up enough for all the responsibility of this.

**Anita** But I'm supposed to be?

**Sam** You're better at it than me.

**Anita** Sam, it's . . . it's just the boil under your arm making you talk like this.

**Sam** This is how I feel most of the time. It's got nothing to do with the fucking boil.

*She is about to attach new dressing.*

**Anita**  It's coming to a head.

**Sam**  Is it?

**Anita**  Definitely.

*Their faces very close together. He puts arm around her. They cuddle.*

**Sam**  Sorry, Anita. Just the job, sort of getting me down. Taking it out on you. Giving, giving, giving all the time at work . . . and when I get home, with you I don't seem to have anything left to give. Just want to take, take, take.

*He helps her attach elastoplast.*

I don't know what I'm hearing half the time. Think I might ask the doctor to give me ears a syringe.

**Anita**  Why?

**Sam**  Pardon?

*She laughs.*

**Anita**  Wish you didn't think so much about everything Sam.

**Sam**  That's what Philip said last night.

**Anita**  So you were out with Philip last night, was you?

**Sam**  Yeah –

**Anita**  Till the pubs closed? Good night was it?

**Sam**  After work, a couple of beers with Philip.

**Anita**  So that's where all the money goes. When was the last time you took me out for a drink?

**Sam**  You never want to go out for a –

**Anita**  Glad you're writing a book of poetry –

**Sam**  A?

**Anita**  To pay for the debts. You pissing all your wages up the wall in the pub with Philip having a good time.

**Sam**  For Christ's sake. Going for a drink with Philip after work – that's not a good time, that's like an alcoholic's course in aversion therapy. I was just killing time with him before a home call –

**Anita**  I bet.

**Sam**  I'm telling you. One of me cases.

**Anita**  Friday night?

**Sam**  Friday night, yeah. She was upset and so –

**Anita**  A *she* was it?

**Sam**  Yes, as a matter of fact. A she.

**Anita**  I see.

**Sam**  What's that supposed to mean?

**Anita**  Nothing.

**Sam**  Good.

**Anita**  Enjoyed yourselves, did you? The pair of you. You and her.

**Sam**  I'm sorry to disappoint you, but unfortunately it wasn't an unpleasant evening.

**Anita**  And you staggered in at midnight, after I'd been here the whole night on me own.

**Sam**  It was me job, work for God's sake.

**Anita**  Until the pubs closed?

**Sam**  She was very upset.

**Anita**  So you come home pissed?

**Sam**  I wasn't pissed. Just not co-ordinating properly

**Anita**  You was sick when you got in. I heard you. You sounded like the Niagara Falls practising.

**Sam**  Give over, Anita. How often do I have a night out? I go out once in a blue moon on a Friday night, just having a couple of jars with a girl who's –

**Anita**  Girl who's what? Who is this mystery woman?

**Sam**  The girl I told you about – whose baby's been taken into care. One of my referrals.

**Anita**  Oh, that cow. Who let her baby set fire to her hands on the electric fire –

**Sam**  An accident –

**Anita**  What's that mean? It didn't hurt the kid?

**Sam**  She lost the kid –

**Anita**  I don't know how you could sit down . . . sit down and drink with a bitch like that. On a Friday night! In a pub.

**Sam**  She's very mixed up.

**Anita**  And it took you till the pub closed to sort her out, did it?

**Sam**  As a matter of fact, it did take that long.

**Anita**  Till the pub closed?

**Sam**  Yes!

**Anita**  Then what did you do?

**Sam**  I drove her home.

**Anita**  Drove her home? What in – not our car?

**Sam**  No, not our car. The office car.

**Anita**  The office car? You borrowed the office car for her?

**Sam**  I borrowed the office car . . . yesterday afternoon. No, not just for her –

**Anita**  But you drove her home in it?

**Sam**  I drove her home in it.

**Anita**  So you admit it! Didn't it seem odd?

**Sam**  Odd, how do you mean, odd?

**Anita**  A bit peculiar. Driving her home.

**Sam**  No, it didn't seem peculiar. In no way peculiar.

**Anita**  How peculiar, that you didn't find it peculiar. Where's she live?

**Sam**  The exact address?

**Anita**  Squat or mobile home?

**Sam**  With her mother and step-father, actually.

**Anita**  Oh, *actually*. What's her name – this step-daughter you find so interesting. What's her name? Surely you called her something.

**Sam**  Karen.

**Anita**  That's what you called her? Karen?

**Sam**  I couldn't call her 'Oi You', could I.

**Anita**  So while you were calling her Karen . . . what did she call you?

**Sam**  Guess.

*Pause.* **Anita** *tries to roll herself a cigarette. She's not good at this.*

**Anita**  Karen, Karen . . . that's a nice name. Sort of name of someone who'd drink . . . pernod and blackcurrant. Is that what she drunk?

**Sam**  What is this?

**Anita**  Just showing an interest in your work. Your cases . . . what pub did you go to?

**Sam**  The Cranbrook, in Ilford.

**Anita**  The Cranbrook, in Ilford? I thought everyone from the centre goes to the –

**Sam**  That's why I didn't take her there. That's why I drove her to Ilford. Because I didn't want everyone from the office leering at her.

**Anita**  Oh, so she's attractive then, is she?

*Pause.*

Well?

**Sam**  As a matter of fact –

**Anita**  As a matter of fact, what?

**Sam**  She is very attractive.

*Pause. She gets* **Sam** *to roll the cigarette.*

**Anita**  That surprises me. That she spent so much time with you, on a Friday night, if she's attractive. In what way is she attractive?

**Sam**  She's 19. She's got long blonde hair and brown eyes, enormous brown eyes. And an almost translucent skin. And she's slim and quite tall and she wears short skirts, they're short in a way that accentuates the length and the shape and the splendour of her almost schoolgirl thighs. You expect her to have playground scars on her knees. She's got freckles sort of scattered about her nose, and her teeth are very white and spaced sort of unexpectedly regularly. She's got big tits.

**Anita**  And she let her baby nearly burn itself to death?

**Sam**  That's not what happened –

**Anita**  It was taken away –

**Sam**  An interim care order was put on the baby. She was very upset. That's why I took her for a drink last night –

**Anita**  And you enjoyed it?

**Sam**  Yeah, I admit it. I did enjoy her company as a matter of fact

**Anita**  Better than mine?

**Sam**  I didn't say that.

**Anita**  Better than mine?

**Sam**  It was a nice change. All right?

**Anita**  Talking about neglecting babies?

**Sam**  She wanted to talk about –

**Anita**  The two of your have got a lot in common.

**Sam**  She wanted to talk . . . let it out. So I could understand her feelings –

**Anita**  I bet you understood. 'Cause you'd kill Katey.

**Sam**  Don't be stupid.

**Anita**  Yes, that's what you'd like to do. Bet you and her had a good old chin wag about that. Good job they took it away, before she does kill it.

**Sam**  She doesn't want to kill it. She wants the kid back!

**Anita**  Is that how she lied to you? You believed her?

**Sam**  She was crying.

**Anita**  That's the oldest trick in the book. Dance with her, did you? I know what the Cranbrook used to be like. Lights dimmed the last hour and smooching –

**Sam**  Okay, so we did have a dance.

**Anita**  What record was they playing?

**Sam**  Does this fucking matter?

**Anita**  What record?

**Sam**  Otis Redding, I think.

**Anita**  Too busy dancing with her to notice.

**Sam**  She was crying. I was trying to comfort her a bit before I drove her home.

**Anita**  In the office car? When you got her home – park outside her house did you?

**Sam**  No, at the bottom of her road I opened the door and chucked her out.

**Anita**  Did you kiss her?

**Sam**  Anita . . .

**Anita**  Did you switch off the engine, and in the dark, put your arm around her . . . and kiss her?

*Pause.*

Did you? I don't mind. Just tell me. Was it nice? Did it seem peculiar, kissing someone else? Is she a better kisser than me?

**Sam** *pulls on sweater.*

**Anita**  I'm asking you – did you like kissing her better than me?

**Sam** *evades her.*

**Anita**  Well?

**Sam**  I didn't kiss her.

**Anita**  Bet you did. Bet you did more than that. Bet she led you on. Not that you'd have needed it. She sounds exactly the sort of slut who'd –

**Sam**  She's not a slut.

**Anita**  Slag. I can smell her scent on you. Slag.

**Sam**  Don't call her a slag.

**Anita**  Karen sounds like a slag's name. How old did you say the slag is? She sounds disgusting. I bet everyone in the pub thought: who's that young slag with that dirty old man with boils! I bet they all thought she was disgusting. You should have told her you're married –

**Sam**  I did.

**Anita**  You talked about me to her?

**Sam**  I said I was married.

**Anita**  Did you have it off with her?

*Pause.*

Did you?

*Pause.*

Did you want to?

*Pause.*

Would she have let you fuck her?

*Pause.* **Anita** *starts to cry.* **Sam** *puts on shoes.*

I don't mind. Honest I don't even if you did. Sam, where are you going?

*She blocks doorway.*

**Sam**  I'm taking the slag to the children's home in Beckenham.

**Anita**  Our car don't work – me brother hasn't fixed it yet.

**Sam**  In the office car. She's got visiting rights. I'm taking her this morning to introduce her to the people who run the home.

**Anita**  Please don't go, Sam. You can't leave me on me own. Not on a Saturday. Me mum's looking after Katey. So we can be on our own today, might be last chance before Cyril comes . . . please, phone up Philip ask him to go with her instead . . . you can't drive with your boil . . .

*She clings to him. He's embarrassed, trying to shake her off.*

Please don't go, Sam. We could go to bed this afternoon. Come to bed with me this afternoon. You always used to like it in the afternoon. I'll put on stockings. I know you must have been missing it. We can go to bed this afternoon and –

**Sam** *closes door.*

**Anita**  I'll let you come up my arse . . .

*Alone she starts to cry, tries to roll a cigarette and fails. All this as Otis Redding's* Try a Little Tenderness *plays.*

# Act Two

Scene Three

*Evening.* East Enders *theme tune as lights up to reveal* **Anita** *sitting on sofa, watching old black and white TV. She wears mock fur coat inside out, woollen tea cosy hat, football socks. Room very untidy.*
*Enter* **Sam** *in a rage wearing coat.*

**Sam**  And now someone's nicked the bloody wheels.

*No reaction from* **Anita**.

From the Escort. From the office car – all the bloody wheels have been nicked.

**Sam** *bellows at* **Anita** *who continues to stare at TV as theme tune fades and dialogue begins.*

Propped up on bricks. All the wheels gone.

**Anita**  When you say *all* the wheels, do you mean even the steering wheel?

**Sam**  No, I don't mean the steering wheel. I mean the four *exterior* wheels. It was when I started the engine with me hands on the unstolen steering wheel that I discovered –

**Anita**  Me brother said you needed locking nuts on Escort wheels. He told you someone'd have them if you left it outside here.

**Sam**  Coming to something when you can't leave the office car outside for half an hour without having the wheels nicked. And your own car without it being pelted with tomatoes again. Why didn't they nick the wheels off the VW that don't work?

**Anita**  Me brother got it working.

*She dangles car keys.*

**Sam**  It's working?

**Anita**  Yeah, he came round this afternoon and got it working.

**Sam**  And it works?

**Anita**  He said you've got a good little runner there.

**Sam**  I told you it was a bargain. What was wrong with it? Sparking plugs?

**Anita**　No petrol.

**Sam**　What?

**Anita**　No petrol in it. That was all that was the matter.

**Sam**　Well, that's handy –

**Anita**　He put in a can. That was all that was the matter with it –

**Sam**　Amazing. I checked the plugs, I checked the battery, oil filter and . . . needn't have borrowed the office car after all. Hassle it was getting it off Philip tonight –

**Anita**　Have you quite finished?

**Sam**　A?

**Anita**　Cause I'm watching the telly. Do you mind?

**Sam**　What's the matter, Anita?

**Anita**　I'm trying to watch the telly.

**Sam**　Interesting?

**Anita**　Maybe. Heard a rumour Pat might smile tonight – I don't want to miss that.

**Sam**　What's up Anita?

**Anita**　Up, up? I'm having a lovely time. Wish you was here.

**Sam**　You look terrible.

**Anita**　I'm trying to improve my IQ.

**Sam**　If you're not careful, you're going to start getting nits in your hair. When was the last time you washed it . . . brushed it?

**Anita**　I can't remember. What's the point anyway?

**Sam**　Anita, what are you doing to yourself? You're letting yourself go.

**Anita**　Then why don't you write up a report about me? 'Noticed she hasn't washed her hair for a week.'

**Sam**　Why?

*He takes hold of her.*

**Anita**　Take your hands off me, take your filthy hands off me. Don't touch me. You're hurting me.

*She punches his arm.*

You're hurting me. Let go.

*He releases her.*

Thank you.

**Sam**  What's going on Anita? Place looks like a bomb's hit it. You flopping around all the time in bloody old coat inside out, me old football socks . . . same old flannelette nightgown morning, noon and night –

**Anita**  It's cold in here, haven't you noticed? If you was here more often you'd notice. It's very cold in here.

**Sam**  Then wear a different old coat and a different pair of football socks and a different flannelette nighty. Besot me with variety. Comb your bloody hair. Wash it.

**Anita**  I did the other day.

**Sam**  Bit of style, touch of the Sunsilk TV commercials, so airline pilots say to each other: 'Fuck this flying the Concorde lark: the important question is – is she wearing Harmony hair lacquer?'

**Anita**  No I'm not. I don't feel like it.

**Sam**  You don't seem to feel like nothing. I know Cyril's a week overdue, but you should be –

**Anita**  How should I be? This is interesting. Please tell me. 'Cause you're a man. So you tell me. How should I be feeling? I only know how I *do* feel.

**Sam**  What I mean is –

**Anita**  Go on, tell me. I'm curious. I want to know. It might help me feel better if you tell me, as an expert on being pregnant – I'm only a woman and I feel very unhappy with the way I feel and I need to hear from you, a man, exactly –

**Sam**  OK, point taken, I got it darling. But it does occur to me that you might feel a little bit better if you –

**Anita**  Change me hairstyle?

**Sam**  Well –

**Anita**  Bit of mascara, eye shadow? That'll make me feel better. Like me ankles'll stop feeling so swollen, as if I'm wearing water wings in my socks and breasts so heavy, and knife in me back, and

I can't sleep. I crash out before ten o'clock, then boing! Two hours later wide awake. Scoffing Marmite sandwiches till I feel sick and feeling so dirty, and ugly and fat and tired and –

**Sam**  You weren't like this when you had Kate.

**Anita**  You were different then. We had Kate together. You were all over me. You couldn't help me enough. We *shared* having Kate. Now you've left me to feel so much on me own.

**Sam**  I think you're getting things out of proportion. Being nostalgic about –

**Anita**  Maybe I am. 'Cause then I really did think you wanted a baby with me. Now –

**Sam**  Now what?

**Anita**  Now I'm not so sure . . .

*Pause.*

I keep having this nightmare, Sam. It keeps coming. It's so vivid, so real I could touch it. It's snowing, it's cold . . . we're looking for somewhere to live. But no one will have us because of the children. They see me holding Katey and Cyril and the pram outside piled high with saucepans and bags with our clothes and we're walking and walking . . . looking at the adverts on the postcards in the newsagents' windows and . . . everytime we get to one of the flats advertised, they see me and Katey and Cyril and they say . . . it's gone. So in the end, you say: let's get a mortgage and buy somewhere. And we go into the Woolwich, and you fill in the form . . . everyone looking at us . . . and the man behind the counter, when he looks at what you've written down – he starts laughing. And everyone starts laughing. Great loud laughing. And you walk out, just leave me standing there with Katey and Cyril as everyone's laughing. And I'm watching you through the window, with everyone laughing. And I see you jump on a Green Line Bus. And it drives off.

**Sam**  Where to?

**Anita**  Basildon.

**Sam**  Why Basildon?

**Anita**  That's where it said it was going. On the front of the bus.

*Pause.*

**Sam**  Anita. I hope this reassures you. I wouldn't be seen dead in Basildon. Stop worrying – everything's going to work out all right.

**Anita**  That's all you ever say. Have you seen the electricity bill – final demand?

**Sam**  I've sorted it all out with Charles –

**Anita**  Who's Charles?

**Sam**  Bank manager – very nice fellah, as it turned out.

**Anita**  Father figure?

**Sam**  He's got a sense of humour. I expected someone about fifty – he looks younger than me.

**Anita**  You went to see him?

**Sam**  I went out to lunch with him.

**Anita**  He took you out to lunch?

**Sam**  Nar, I took him. Quite an interesting moment, watching his face when it came to me signing the cheque to pay the bill. I mentioned to the waiter that he was my bank manager. He could hardly bounce the cheque after that, could he.

**Anita**  You're irresponsible!

**Sam**  He didn't seem to think so. He's as pissed off with flash Yuppies as we are. Thinks I'm underpaid and a bit of a saint. Too unwordly to handle money matters, as long as we don't go more than a grand overdrawn, no problem. Didn't even want to see evidence of our collateral.

**Anita**  We haven't got any.

**Sam**  He seemed to assume we had a mortgage, man in my position with an MA. We sorted out a monthly budget account to pay the bills as they come in. And I get the cheque from the publishers for the book of poems.

**Anita**  Why can't you be serious!

**Sam**  I can't be serious when you're being serious, Anita. If we both start to be serious simultaneously, me brain starts to go numb. I start feeling as if I'm wearing the wrong head on me shoulders. As if I'm wearing a head that belongs to someone else.

**Anita**  God, things you say – a conversation with you . . . you make Jehovah's Witnesses and Derek Jameson sound like sane, rational, sensible people. Sam, can't you get it in your thick head that I'm worried to death?

**Sam**  I have gathered that. You've made that clear. But, what you can't seem to see yourself is – because Cyril's overdue, you're over-dramatising everything and getting everything out of proportion.

**Anita**  Bills we can't pay, getting more and more in debt, everything getting worse . . .

**Sam**  The bills are getting paid. We're only a grand in debt. I've applied for an Access card, so with Charles's help we should be able to run up another seven hundred and fifty credit.

**Anita**  We used to have money in the building society. Earning interest. When you was at University. When you weren't earning anything.

**Sam**  You were. And we had no responsibilities.

**Anita**  We was saving up for a mortgage. I thought when you qualified and got a job we'd get one.

**Sam**  So did I.

**Anita**  We used to go out then.

**Sam**  Yeah.

**Anita**  At least one night a week.

**Sam**  I know.

**Anita**  Parties.

**Sam**  People we knew used to have parties then. Now everyone's got kids, don't have parties now.

**Anita**  Used to go out for a meal.

**Sam**  Restaurant prices are crazy now –

**Anita**  To the cinema. Used to see a lot of films . . .

**Sam**  Yeah.

**Anita**  And to the theatre. We used to see a lot of plays.

**Sam**  Yeah.

**Anita**  I miss that.

**Sam**  Things used to be a lot cheaper.

**Anita**  When I look through me brother's *Time Out* now, at all what's on in London – it's like a different planet.

**Sam**  Everything costs so much now.

**Anita**  The thing I think I miss most, is not going to gigs anymore. When was the last time we –

**Sam**  Woolwich Town Hall, the Thursday night before Katey was born.

**Anita**  Woolwich Town Hall.

**Sam**  Eddy Floyd.

**Anita**  Hardly anyone there.

**Sam**  Wasn't he great.

**Anita**  He made it like . . . he was just doing it for us. Everything we asked him to sing –

**Sam**  The Otis Redding –

**Anita**  That was a great night.

**Sam**  Yeah.

*Silence.*

**Anita**  What are you thinking, Sam?

**Sam**  Thinking how everything was so different, just that short time ago.

**Anita**  Ten months?

**Sam**  I felt so full of hope . . that I was achieving something. Could help people. Could get the homeless a home, and little victories . . . could get them furniture and cookers and – and not being despised. This nosey parker, busy body the council sent along. Not surprised we're hated so much, despised, mistrusted so much – why do we keep poking our nose in when there's nothing tangible we can do?

**Anita**  I wish you cared about trying to do something for me and Katey and Cyril here as you do about those other people.

**Sam**  Such as, what can I do?

**Anita**  You could do what Ronnie did!

**Sam**  No. I am not, never, ever going to sell out like Ronnie. Why should I be run out of London?

**Anita**  Because we can't afford a decent life here.

**Sam**  So go and run a fucking old people's home?

**Anita**  Ronnie and Jean have got a nice place to live. A better standard of living. They're not poor, poor, poor.

**Sam**  I don't want that, Anita.

**Anita**  Why?

**Sam**  Because it's giving up, that's why.

**Anita**  But we can't afford it here, Sam. And this is the poorest part of London. We can't carry on like this – not with children and responsibilities. We're never going to buy any house if we stay here. We'll always be . . . dying of drafts and damp rot, wallpaper peeling and no hot water without the Ascot exploding and . . . never no summer holidays or a car that don't break down or . . . I want nice things. Just to be normal. I'm not asking for paradise.

*Pause.*

It's dangerous here. And I hate being so poor. It's making me miserable. It's changing me. I don't want to live like this anymore.

**Sam**  What do you want me to do? Become a Yuppie, city whizz kid? Something like that?

**Anita**  I'd hate you if you did, not that you could. Same job. Just somewhere else, like what Ronnie –

*Silence.*

Think about it . . . maybe we could drive down to Suffolk and see what –

**Sam**  I've got work to do.

**Anita**  Tonight? You never work on a Tuesday night –

**Sam**  It's the only night she can –

*Pause.*

**Anita**  Her again? Karen?

**Sam**  It was the only night I could get an appointment with her. A psychiatrist who specialises in –

**Anita**  Couldn't someone else take her? You're not the only bloody social worker there.

**Sam**  She's *my* case.

**Anita**  (*cool*)  Would you mind if she wasn't?

*Pause.*

Would you.

**Sam**  I dunno.

**Anita**  Sam, what is it about her?

*Pause.*

Because, admit it . . . you don't have to see her as often as you do see her . . .

**Sam**  No.

**Anita**  Why do you then?

*Pause.*

She's got you bad, hasn't she, Sam?

**Sam**  I can't understand it Anita.

**Anita**  Try to explain.

**Sam**  I can't. She's just a kid. It don't make any sense. Feel, she needs me. Makes such a change, a client who needs me –

**Anita**  It's more than that.

**Sam**  Then started feeling . . . for her . . . wish to Christ I didn't Anita. Sorry.

*He reaches for her.*

**Anita**  Don't touch me. It's vile, it's disgusting –

**Sam**  No, just some moment of irrational –

**Anita**  I don't want to hear any more about it.

**Sam**  I love you . . . this is just some weird infatuation or something . . . I don't understand it.

**Anita**  I don't want to hear about it. Please don't tell me about it.

**Sam**  She . . . I was trying to avoid her . . . but she

*Pause.*

She needs me. Or think she needs me. Someone stable.

**Anita**  Stable, you?

**Sam**  In her eyes . . . I tried to avoid her but –

*Pause.*

Now I can't. It's just a temporary thing –

**Anita**  And you've been sleeping in here on the sofa every night this week . . . do I revolt you? Don't you want to sleep in the same bed as me anymore?

**Sam**  I don't know how I feel, Anita, something weird's going on in me head. I feel like I'm wearing someone else's head. Please cuddle me –

**Anita**  Ask the slag.

**Sam**  Please –

**Anita**  Does she know I'm having another baby?

**Sam**  Yes. She asks every time I –

**Anita**  How can you talk about me to her?

**Sam**  Because I love you.

**Anita**  You'd better go then. Don't keep her waiting. She might find someone else.

**Sam**  Anita. Please help me.

**Anita**  Help you! Ask her! Shall I be like here? Shall I do what she nearly let happen . . . kill a baby? Like her! Kill my baby . . . like her . . . like she nearly killed her baby . . . I'll kill mine then . . .

**Sam** *turns away as she begins to violently bash her fists into her bulging belly.*

**Sam**  Don't be mad –

**Anita**  It's you who's mad, not me.

*She grabs large table lamp. Before* **Sam** *can prevent her, she smashes it into her stomach, breaking the lamp bulb. Then she groans loudly in darkened room.*

**Sam**  Anita . . .

*She groans again and slumps to the floor.*

Anita?

*He kneels beside her.*

**Anita** Christ, Sam . . .

*He hugs her. She groans again.*

**Sam** Jesus.

**Anita** I can feel it coming down me legs.

**Sam** A?

**Anita** I can feel it running down me legs . . . what colour is it Sam?

**Sam** You want me to have a look?

**Anita** What colour is it Sam?

**Sam** It's sort of . . . it's hard to describe . . .

**Anita** Not blood?

**Sam** No, not blood.

*He leans her down, raises her nightdress and fingers between her legs and then inspects his fingers.*

**Sam** More like . . . water.

**Anita** I'm not bleeding?

**Sam** No, more like water.

*She groans again.*

**Anita** Don't go Sam.

**Sam** Rolling pin . . . bang on the floor so . . . get the midwife.

**Anita** Not enough time, not now Sam. Broken the bag, that's what I've done, that's what happening . . . you'll have to help me. Show you what to do . . .

**Sam** You just tell me what to do . . . sorry, I don't know what to do. Think at school in domestic science – think they'd teach the lads how to do a baby birth as well as rustle up a fucking pizza.

**Anita** Stop panicking . . . help me, help me. Hot water and –

**Sam** Towels? Hot water and towels . . . it's all coming to me now . . . You wait there . . .

*He dashes into kitchen. She groans and shouts as she starts pressing. He dashes back with towels.*

The fucking Ascot's broken again. I'll fix it on Saturday. I've put the kettle on.

**Sam** Here . . . you know what we're supposed to be doing?

**Anita** Ought to. I've done it before.

*She laughs. He laughs. She groans. As she screams, he hammers the floor with a shoe.*

**Sam** So she'll phone the midwife . . . I don't want to do nothing wrong . . .

*The following dialogue at intervals as* **Sam** *helps* **Anita**.

**Sam** Your teeth are chattering.

**Anita** Oh God, Oh Jesus . . . everything's going tight Sam.

**Sam** Just keep telling me what to do . . .

**Anita** It's happening so quickly, oh Jesus . . . so quickly.

**Sam** Everything's all right! Don't worry, relax. I'm here. Everything's all right. Is everything all right? It is, isn't it?

**Anita** Sam, can you see . . . look.

**Sam** Oh Christ.

**Anita** Can you see.

*He peers up her nightdress.*

**Sam** Oh, looks like he's got dark hair.

**Anita** Not *his* hair you fucking idiot. Not . . . God, God.

*She alternates laughs with shouts as she pushes.*

**Sam** Keep going, princess – you're nearly there.

**Anita** Tickling me now . . .

**Sam** You're brilliant at this . . . just a bit more . . .

**Anita** Look at me, Sam. I feel so beautiful . . .

**Sam** You are. You look so beautiful . . .

*More groans.*

**Anita** Do I really?

**Sam** So very, very beautiful . . .

*They embrace.*
*Blackout.*

Scene Four

*Evening. Room very tidy and table centre of room laid for dinner: candle in bottle, small vase of flowers, two chairs facing each other. Birthday cards on mantlepiece. Wrapped presents on table.* **Sam** *enters. He notices the table spread. Goes to bedroom door.*

**Anita** (*from bedroom*)  No don't come in! I'm not ready yet. You're early.

**Sam**  You said don't be late.

**Anita**  Earlier than I expected.

**Sam**  Who you got in there?

**Anita**  Bloke from Squeeze. I thought you'd go for a drink after work.

**Sam**  Was going to . . . but this afternoon, one of the best things that's happened for ages happened

**Anita**  Sshh!

**Sam** *wanders around room, starts feeling presents as* **Anita** *comes out of bedroom. Now no longer pregnant, she looks beautiful in a nice dress and hair and eyes made up. She approaches* **Sam** (*fiddling with his birthday presents*) *from behind. She pinches his buttocks. Then they kiss.*

**Anita**  You sounded ever so pleased about something –

**Sam**  I am bloody pleased. It's one of those things that makes it all worth while. Something achieved for a change! It's about the best buzz we've all had since we were involved in the decanting of Ronan Point – Philip keeps going on about it, donkey's years ago when –

**Anita**  I know. You really do look so . . . tell me?

**Sam**  It's nothing much . . . just a titchy little victory, but so rewarding . . .

*During this* **Sam** *has taken off coat, now listens at bedroom door, opens it a few inches, peers in.*

If I kiss them goodnight, I might wake Lucy up . . .

**Anita**  I think our Lucy will wake up before long anyway . . .

**Sam**  I'll wait till she wakes up then.

**Anita**  Go on, tell me.

*He sits at table. She serves nibbles.*

**Sam**  Well, it's gonna sound so trivial but –

**Anita**  Yes?

**Sam**  Well, the other day . . . there was this mother of a travelling family got arrested for assaulting a policeman. Usual thing, but – a son with her when they arrested her. About six or seven. Was put into custody overnight, so we got the kid into care with a foster mother . . . she was remanded in custody for a week when she come up in court this morning . . . she wouldn't give her address, the father's . . . nor would the kid. Then the foster mother phones up and says . . . the kid has stolen all her jewellery. When we got there he half undressed himself, hollering 'I haven't got it, I haven't got nothing, search me.' Her rings and watch and other bits were in his socks of course. To calm him down a bit, took him for a drive and he suddenly says: 'I want to be with my dad'. I said: 'Do you know where he is.' He said ''Course I know where he is, he's my dad!' So I drove him to where he said, and there he was. So now he's not in care.

*He laughs.*

Don't sound much put it like that, but –

**Anita**  Happy birthday, Sam

*They kiss.*

Didn't say it to you properly this morning when you went out. I was dopey.

**Sam**  Rotten night.

**Anita**  I don't mind if our Lucy cries all night every night. Just so glad she's all right.

**Sam**  You look lovely. So fabulous . . .

**Anita**  Do I?

**Sam**  If you weren't a married woman . . . I wouldn't be able to keep me hands off you.

**Anita**  I won't tell him.

*They kiss and he runs hands over her breasts.*

**Anita**  I feel nice. I feel so much better than I did. I felt so ugly.

**Sam**  You didn't look it. You looked so lovely.

**Anita**  You always said it was a myth pregnant women look attractive. Just an old wive's tale, a rumour that's put around to cheer up the poor cows.

**Sam**  I said that?

**Anita**  Years ago.

**Sam**  Just a joke.

**Anita**  You meant it.

**Sam**  I didn't know what I was talking about . . . hadn't seen you pregnant then.

**Anita**  Let's get this out of the way – I want to say sorry about how bad I was, being so difficult.

**Sam**  You weren't.

**Anita**  I was. I was bad.

**Sam**  You weren't, I'm telling you, but even if you had been – not without reason, all that hanging around waiting.

**Anita**  Then clever old you, being here when it mattered, doing the business.

**Sam**  You told me how to –

**Anita**  I couldn't have done it on me own.

**Sam**  Nor could I.

**Anita**  I'd always regretted you weren't at Katey's birth, there with me. Like they all say – father present, it really unites a man and his wife. Never sure whether I believed it until . . . well, we went one better didn't we, with Lucy? Really together for keeps now Sam.

**Sam**  Not arf.

**Anita**  Things I said that night . . . things that came out –

**Sam**  Think you were bursting to let them out, had to come out sooner or later.

*To avoid this conversation, he goes to bedroom door and opens it again. Listens.*

Can just hear them breathing . . .

**Anita**  I was really scared of losing you.

*Pause.*

To that girl.

**Sam**  Well, you shouldn't have been. Fag?

**Anita**  Have one of these.

**Sam**  Bensons?

**Anita**  Why not. After all, it is your birthday.

*She takes pack of ten from drawer. She declines cigarette he offers her.*

**Anita**  Nar, not now. I'll have one after supper. Cut right down now, then pack it up altogether.

**Sam**  It's a mug's game. (*He inhales luxuriously.*) I'm on the brink of starting to cut down meself . . .

**Anita**  And then stop altogether?

**Sam**  Hang on, moderation in everything I say.

*She laughs.*

**Anita**  We'll arf save a lot of money, if I just stop. Three quid a week –

**Sam**  Me, more –

**Anita**  I'd better see how the meal's getting on. Reckon on you being another half hour –

**Sam**  I did see Ronnie, if that's what you're wondering.

**Anita**  Ronnie, oh him –

**Sam**  Yes him.

*Pause.*

**Anita**  I got a bottle of wine, why don't you open it and –

*She hands bottle and corkscrew to him.*

**Sam**  *opens the bottle. He pours into both the glasses on the dinner table.*

**Anita**  Cheers then.

**Sam**  Cheers.

**Anita**  Happy birthday.

*They sip wine.*

**Anita**  Nice one –

**Sam**  Good choice.

**Anita**  I'm not much of a –

**Sam**  Really?

**Anita**  You're the expert on –

**Sam**  Yeah I suppose I am.

*Pause.*

**Anita**  Your present! Two presents! This one is from me mum and brother and me . . . this is just from me.

**Sam**  What one shall I open first?

**Anita**  That one. Me mum and me brother and –

*He opens the bigger, the bulkier package. A suede jacket.*

**Sam**  A suede jacket.

**Anita**  Do you like it? Try it on. If it don't fit or if you don't like –

*He tries it on. Struts, looks in mirror.*

**Sam**  Wait till fucking Harry sees this!

**Anita**  What do you think?

**Sam**  (*nods, pleased; looking at himself in mirror*)  I think I'll take the job Ronnie offered . . .

*Pause.*

Makes sense. Makes sense. There's no future here. Way things are. I've done three years and . . . no one else has done four years.

**Anita**  I admit I wrote to Jane and him to –

**Sam**  Glad you did. We owe it to the girls. Better start in life, grow up in the country.

**Anita**  It's up to you, Sam. I wrote to him, asked him to see you so you'd . . . I was so confused at the time, that week – wanted you to think about it seriously.

**Sam**  Only took a minute. About the time it takes to father a baby . . . I think I'd decided anyway . . . hoping against hope that something would happen to decide me to stay.

**Anita**  Honestly, cause –

**Sam**  When they erected the iron bars over the windows – I thought: us here in this building are here to help. Now we need protection.

**Anita**  Yes?

**Sam**  Vivid moments like that. When Aysha got beaten up in the pub. 'Why, why?' No idea Philip said. Could be just because she's Asian – or they might have done it because she's a social worker. He wasn't at all surprised when I handed in me notice this afternoon.

*Pause. She refills her glass.*

Yes, I told him. Said he was surprised I lasted so long. Said he'd do it himself if he was younger. I put in in writing. He said, sleep on it tonight – give it to him in the morning. Suddenly he looked so old. So . . .

*He has pulled letter from pocket. She doesn't look at it. Feels the other parcel. Places letter on table.*

This feels like a record . . . your present.

**Anita**  Just from me.

**Sam**  Glad I've done it?

**Anita**  Only if you are.

**Sam**  You're the sensible one. Feet on the ground. Me – must be round the bend to have wanted to be a social worker in the first place. (*Opens present.*) Great. (*Inspects titles on album cover.*) Can I put it on . . .

*He places record on turntable.*

Come on, let's have a dance . . . These are the ones we used to dance to –

*Waits for intro of first track.*

**Anita**  That's why I bought it for you – stupid fucker!

*Record plays: Ronnettes* Baby I Love You. *They both dance and sing along to it, lighthearted – like the first time they met. They kiss.* **Anita** *stops record.*

**Anita**  This is why I bought it, thought – this side.

**Sam**  They're all great. It's a great album –

**Anita**  While I dish up the food . . . this side . . . this one you asked

Eddie Floyd to sing . . . the record that was on the first time we –

**Sam**  Otis Redding. *My Girl.*

**Anita**  Am I still?

*Pause.*

**Sam**  I'll put it on.

**Anita**  I'm sure we've done the right thing. So nice to see you so happy for a change . . .

*He places stylus on track and she goes into kitchen.* **Sam**'s *mood changes as intro of* My Girl *begins to play. He sits at table, opens envelope of resignation letter and reads it. He begins to cry as Otis sings. The kitchen door opens.* **Anita** *is about to bring in food. She sees* **Sam** *crying. She hesitates, then she backs into kitchen and closes door.*

**Sam** *alone as record continues and lights fade.*

# Frozen Assets

**Frozen Assets** was commissioned and first performed by the
Royal Shakespeare Company at the Warehouse Theatre, London
on 9 January 1978 with the following cast:

| | |
|---|---|
| **Buddy** | Allan Hendrick |
| **Screw** | David Waller |
| **Auntie Connie** | Ruby Head |
| **Pam** | Marjorie Bland |
| **Ronnie** | David Howey |
| **Frank** | Martin Read |
| **Joan** | Marilyn Goldsworthy |
| **Al** | Fred Molina |
| **Priest** | John Nettles |
| **Dave** | Kevin O'Shea |
| **Sammy** | Clyde Pollitt |
| **Edna** | Denyse Alexander |
| **Henry** | Martin Read |
| **Lord Plaistow** | David Waller |
| **Peter** | John Nettles |

*Director*   Barry Kyle
*Designer*   Sally Gardner

# Act One

*Music before play: The Band's* Christmas Must Be Tonight, *from the album* Islands.

*Empty stage, cold winter light, a dirty plank set stage right. A dead duck set centre upstage. And a football. Music fades. Sound of wind.* **Buddy** *enters, shivering with the cold. About 17, with short Borstal hair and Borstal uniform: blue and white pin-striped shirt, plimsolls and jeans too short in the leg and too large at the waist; he has tightened the waistband with large safety pins.*

*He shivers, rubs his shoulders to keep warm.*

**Buddy** Shit. Ball in the river. Stuck on the ice. If it was a goal everytime someone kicked it in the river, we'd run up a landslide against them village poufs.

*He pauses and wonders how to get the ball. Then he dashes off and returns immediately with a spiked pole.*

This's what'll get it. They said I could play football today.

*He gets the plank and rests it across the imaginery river towards the football.*

They promised me. I even got changed, and put on the linseed oil – on me legs. I was all ready to go, then Jamie said his bugger of a leg was better and that he was playing after all. So I put me clothes back on and went behind the goal. I have to get the ball everytime one of them village poufs misses the goal and it comes out here, on the outside. I'm doing more jumping about than our goalie.

*He gingerly balances on the plank with the spike to try and reach the ball. He cannot quite reach it. Instead he spikes the dead duck. He picks up the duck.*

Blimey. Copped it.

**Voice** Clark, Clark!

**Buddy** *is fascinated by the duck as* **Screw**, *the Borstal warder, enters.*

**Screw** Clark, what are you doing out here?

**Buddy** It's a dead duck.

**Screw** Did you kill it?

**Buddy** Kill it? Me? No, 'course not, 'course I never.

**Screw** I'm very glad to hear it. (*Takes duck.*) Little duck out for a walk. Not out to get spliced with a spike by the likes of you.

**Buddy** I know. (*Exaggerated sympathy.*) Poor little duck.

**Screw** Are you taking the piss?

**Buddy** Nar –

**Screw** A lot of people think it's a bit peculiar – a man my age liking ducks.

**Buddy** I like them and all.

**Screw** Ducks never hurt no-one. Give them a pond and a few crusts of bread and they're happy.

**Buddy** This one don't look too happy.

**Screw** It's dead, isn't it! Some people would eat that. Bung it in a stew or something. When I became fond of ducks, I turned vegetarian.

**Buddy** Did you?

**Screw** I would have gone macro-biotic, but me wife put her foot down.

**Buddy** Hard cheese.

**Screw** That's what made her fed up – the cheese all the time, every meal.

**Buddy** Better than eating ducks.

**Screw** Don't know how people can do it. It's a tufted scaup.

**Buddy** A what?

**Screw** Name of the duck. Fresh water variety. You can learn a lot of things from ducks. Like for instance . . . You sure you're not taking the piss?

**Buddy** No, I'm very interested. It's just that I don't know much about them.

**Screw** See, he's in his winter plumage. In the winter it's black and white. In the summer he'd be brown and white. If you're not sure whether it's winter or summer, take a look at a tufted scaup and Bob's Your Uncle.

**Buddy** Thanks for the tip. Poor little thing – lovely looking.

**Screw** Should be in Iceland or somewhere like that, this time of year. A fox must have got it. Or them vicious little bleeders in there. You're Clark aren't you?

**Buddy** Yeah.

**Screw** I thought so. What are you doing outside the permitted perimeter?

**Buddy** I come to get the ball, didn't I. It come out.

**Screw** Better throw it back over the fence and get round there inside ourselves.

**Buddy**, *on the plank, reaches for the ball, holding the* **Screw**'s *hand so that he can stretch further. He retrieves the ball and then throws it off stage.*

**Buddy** They said I could play.

**Screw** In the prestige Christmas match against the village?

**Buddy** But Jamie played, because his leg's better. Smells nice outside here. Better than in there.

**Screw** You're not like a young lag, Clark. I see no deep seated villainy in your eyes. I've got one your age myself.

**Buddy** I only nicked a car.

**Screw** And they put you in there?

**Buddy** I did it a few times. Driving cars is my hobby.

**Screw** I see.

**Buddy** Pity I ain't got one.

**Screw** That would be a bit of a handicap. How long to go?

**Buddy** Four weeks and I'm out.

**Screw** Keep out of trouble.

**Buddy** I am.

**Screw** Don't let no-one rile you. Fuck up your good behaviour.

**Buddy** I ain't been in no trouble since I've been in the nick.

**Screw** Think what it's like out here, out here in the country. Breathe it in. Keep it in your lungs so you can remember in there – amid all the stench of latrines and shit and stale spunk. Remember the smell and the goodness of the world outside the prison. Remember and you will keep out of trouble.

**Buddy** Yes.

**Screw** What can you smell, Clark?

**Buddy** (*deep breath, then*) Trees . . . and a bonfire somewhere. Tree smoke . . . cut grass under the snow . . . animals smell . . . and hay burning? I liked October, when they burned the hay in the evenings in the fields.

**Screw** God honest smells, every one of them. You're shivering.

**Buddy** They wouldn't let me put on me jumper, because it's sport.

**Screw** They're barbaric, some of them, even if I do say it myself. Keep this duck out of their sight. I'll bury it later. See down river? Down stream, by the village. Kids skating on the river, All right, that, eh? When you're free, take up skating and duck watching. Keep you out of trouble.

**Buddy** I will. (*Slight pause.*) There was a duck pond in the park.

**Screw** Eh?

**Buddy** In the park, near home. This man, he fed them. He was mad. They said he was mad. We all walked faster when we passed him in the street. But no need to run – he only had one leg. The other one was wooden.

**Screw** Only having one leg don't mean you're mad. It's like saying if you've got only one arm you're deaf.

**Buddy** Point was: when he walked along, he always kept his hand over his head, like this. (*Places right arm across head.*) So God didn't get his angels to shit on his head.

**Screw** God's got more important things to do with his angels.

**Buddy** And everyone was scared of the madman in the park. I've got toothache.

**Screw** Seen the dentist?

**Buddy** He's off until after Christmas.

**Screw** Bloody typical. Your face looks swollen. Ridiculous in this day and age going round with toothache. I'll give him a phone up for you – get him to look at you this afternoon.

**Buddy** O tar.

*During these last few lines,* **Buddy** *has picked up the plank, holding it dead centre and horizontal to the ground. The* **Screw** *has picked up the spike, its point pointing into his stomach and the other end waist high.* **Buddy** *turns with the plank; the end hammers the spike into the* **Screw**'s *stomach. The* **Screw** *falls to his knees.*

**Buddy**   O Jesus Christ!

**Screw**   You stupid cunt.

**Buddy**   You're all bleeding and bloody.

**Screw**   Get it out! Get it out, you daft prat.

**Buddy**   Accident, only accident, honest. Didn't mean, didn't mean. You're nice to me.

**Screw**   Get this fucking thing out of my guts. Errrrrr.

**Buddy** *tugs at the spike. It snaps in his hands.*

Help, help me. Me whistle, sound the alarm, blow me whistle.

**Buddy** (*shouts*)   Help, help!

**Screw**   Whistle, whistle!

**Buddy**   Where, where?

**Screw**   Pocket, pocket!

**Buddy**   Move over a bit then so that I can –

**Screw**   You fucking daft bleeder.

**Buddy**   Move over and –

**Screw**   You sure you never spiked that duck?

**Buddy**   I promise I never.

**Screw**   Me whistle.

*The* **Screw** *moves over to enable* **Buddy** *to get his hand in to take the whistle.* **Buddy** *blows it – but instead of being a prison whistle it's a duck warbler. He goes to the* **Screw**'*s other pocket. The* **Screw** *lies motionless. He is dead.*

**Buddy**   Got it, get help now. I was only getting the ball. You'll be all right, matey. You won't miss the Christmas carol service. I'll bury the duck and –

*He goes to blow the whistle, but becomes aware of the sudden stiffness of the* **Screw**. *He prods the* **Screw** *with his foot. The* **Screw**'*s arms fall flat.*

O Jesus Christ! O Jesus. You're all right, really you are. You're just a little bit tired. All this fresh air. A bit upset 'cause of the duck getting killed. Having a little rest are you, a little rest? Aren't you. PLEASE. PLEASE. PLEASE SAY YES.

*He looks at the motionless corpse.*

Accident, didn't mean . . . I'm a reformed person. I . . . O . . . Jesus, Jesus, Jesus.

*He blows frenziedly on the whistle again and again.*

*Then, several sirens sound off.* **Buddy** *panics. He goes to dash off, taking the whistle. But he runs back to the duck and takes it as the sirens and alarms reach a crescendo. Blackout. Yellow searchlights comb the auditorium and the sirens continue.*

*Then silence.*

*A misty evening light. The wreck of a car, wheel-less, doorless and rusty. Enter* **Buddy**, *breathless. He leans panting on the wreck of the car.*

**Buddy**  I can still hear the bells ringing in me ears. Like loud pub music – the Boomtown Rats and the Pistols and . . . When you're too near the speaker. And in the quiet outside, you don't know whether you can still really hear it or whether it's just a buzzing in your ears.

*He breathes deeply. Silence. Then a torch on his face and enter* **Connie**, *scruffy, about 60.*

**Connie**  Anyone follow you?

**Buddy**  Nar.

**Connie**  Dogs?

**Buddy**  Nar.

**Connie**  I knew you'd come here. That's why I come here. 'Cause I knew you'd come here. You was mad to come here.

**Buddy**  How did you know I was out?

**Connie**  I heard. Someone told me. I was in the boozer and someone told me. Didn't know it would be you. I come down here and stood watching you and I thought: 'That's my fucking nephew'. I nearly went back to the pub.

**Buddy**  It was good of you to come.

**Connie**  Everyone who breaks out of the prison comes here. For a car. Breakers' yard! Stupid place to come for a motor.

**Buddy**  Got to get out of the area, I've got to.

**Connie**  Don't tell me what you've done. I heard. I said: 'God help the poor little sod when they find him'.

**Buddy**  I got you a duck.

**Connie**  A what?

**Buddy**  A duck. For you.

**Connie**  Thank you, Buddy. That's very nice of you.

**Buddy**  Uncle Harold –

**Connie**  Your Uncle Harold's dead.

**Buddy**  I never knew that.

**Connie**  Didn't your mum write and tell you? Broke his heart when his breathing got so bad. He come here every day.

**Buddy**  I know.

**Connie**  Must have been for . . . fifty years. He loved it here. The yard – it was the love of his life.

**Buddy**  Yeah, I know.

**Connie**  He come down here every day, hell or high water. And at night sometimes. After the pub. To stand here. He said he could hear the horses in the sheds.

**Buddy**  He always liked the horses.

**Connie**  Then he came one day, but he couldn't walk from the bus. He couldn't get here. He got on another bus and came home. He was a broken man. I said: 'What's the matter Harold?' He said: 'I ain't got the breath no more. I couldn't walk to the yard'. (*Pause.*) I miss him.

**Buddy**  I do and all.

**Connie**  That night, I come down here after the funeral. I thought I could hear the horses meself. Mourning for your Uncle Harold. Listen! Wind whistling in the rotting planks of the sheds. Can't you hear it?

**Buddy**  (*pause, then*)  Yeah!

**Connie**  What else can you hear?

**Buddy** *agitated, wants to be off.*

Imagine, can't you. Can't you hear the horses?

**Buddy**  Oh yeah, O yeah. Can hear them.

**Connie**  What are they doing?

**Buddy**  Stamping their hooves. And neighing. And swishing their tails against the walls of the sheds.

**Connie**  You're lying bleeder. There ain't been a horse here since the war.

**Buddy**  I didn't know what to say.

**Connie**  I'm sorry I can't help you, Buddy.

**Buddy**  But Auntie Connie! I'm in trouble.

**Connie**  I can't help you, Buddy. They'll be combing the countryside. I can't hide you here. I ain't got a car here except in hundreds of pieces. This is a breaker's yard now.

**Buddy**  I'm glad you kept the yard

**Connie**  You can have wheels or windows or engines. You can take whatever you like, but none of it works if you ain't got a car to put it in. Sorry, boy. (*Pause.*) Funny, miles from anywhere, and the lights of the prison. See them for miles. Even in the mist. Yellow lights in the orchards.

**Buddy** *strokes the bonnet of a car.* **Connie** *goes to him.*

Funny, a bloke here this morning come in and asked for a carburettor for a Cortina. 'What model?' I said. He said: 'A green one.' (*They both laugh.*) He never cared about cars like you do.

**Buddy**  Yeah, well look where it's got me.

**Connie**  They never come to see me, your family. Even when Harold died, they never come.

**Buddy**  They're a bit funny like that.

**Connie**  Should have come and lived out here in the country. Kept you out of trouble. Away from bad influences.

**Buddy**  There weren't many country boys in there. Still, too late now.

**Connie**  The alarm bells have stopped ringing.

*Silence, they listen.*

**Buddy**  What will I do?

**Connie**  Keep moving. Get to London. There they'll help you.

**Buddy**  I didn't do it on purpose, you know. It was an accident.

**Connie**  Nick a motor from the pub. Half a mile down the road.

**Buddy**  All right.

**Connie**  Want a key?

**Buddy**  Got a hairclip?

**Connie**  You've learned all that then? When it's over . . . come back here. Could use a man who knows about cars. I'll make you a partner.

**Buddy**  All right.

**Connie**  Some clothes. Harold's – in the end shed. Dump the prison clothes somewhere else. Not here. Ssssh . . .

*Sound of a car stopping, off. Headlamps on* **Connie**. **Buddy** *ducks out of sight and crawls off. Dogs bark.*

**Connie** (*calls after* **Buddy**)  Tell your mother, if she'd have come here, you wouldn't be running like a scared rabbit tonight. Quick, go. And tar for the duck.

**Connie** *walks towards the headlamps.*

If you bastards don't get off my late husband's property. I'll blow your heads off with a shotgun.

**Voice**  Police, missus.

**Connie**  Get a search warrant. Go on, prove it. Show your identity. and I'll have to get me reading glasses.

**Connie** *exits. Blackout.*

*Back projection: motorway at night.*
**Buddy** *sits in a car facing the audience.*

**Buddy**  Ice on the road, turn into the skids, turn into the skids. Right mouse holes in this bodywork. Fancy having a nice car and letting it fall to bits. But got a radio.

*He turns on the radio:* Silent Night.
*Another slide of motorway at night.*

Leave the Old Bill tramping round in the slush behind. It'll be closing time before the geezer knows his mother's been nicked then . . . safe. Heart thumping. Nice carol. (*Sings.*) Silent night, Holy night . . . The ones in there, the ones who are alcoholics, they get them off on Jesus. Give them god instead of the Johnny Walker. (*Laugh uncontrollably. Staggers out of car and vomits over bonnet. Pauses.*) Didn't mean it. Didn't mean it. Should have pushed the body in the fucking stream. Tell them it was an accident? What, and have them rattle the cell keys in your mouth? Smash your teeth out? Iron bar up your arsehole? On the fucking man! Ain't like this in Kojak. (*Calms.*) Get home . . . nice cup of tea. Lot of sugar. And this fucking toothache! Tooth stops hurting and everything'll be all right.

*Blackout. Police radio tells of suspect on the run.*

*Lights up on* **Pam** *sitting on an armchair drinking, with a whisky bottle at her foot. An attractive woman, about 28.*

*Singing* Jingle Bells, **Ronnie** *enters, pulling on rail of expensive coats – and a truck laden with TV sets, radios, stereos, parcels wrapped in Christmas paper and handbags. He tries on a full-length leather overcoat.*

**Ronnie**   Well, what do you think?

**Pam**   All right.

**Ronnie**   All right? Is that all you can say? Must be worth over a ton for Christ's sake. Hardly been worn, not a crease.

**Pam**   Yeah. Al phoned. He'll be here with the lorry in half an hour.

**Ronnie**   Good. I wish you'd leave off that for one night, Pam. Especially tonight. Very big night. Makes me nervous. Christ, I can smell you like a distillery when you get out of the lift, let alone in here.

**Pam**   It's Christmas.

**Ronnie**   What about the other three hundred odd nights?

**Pam**   Practising for Christmas.

**Ronnie**   Yeah.

*He takes out an electronic calculator and begins to evaluate coats. She fingers the parcels.*

**Pam**   Shall I open them?

**Ronnie**   Nar, leave them. Leave them, will you!

**Pam**   Might be something I'm after. Some Joy perfume or something. Only sniffing.

**Ronnie**   Leave them, Pam. I said leave them. (*Grabs her arm.*)

**Pam**   You're hurting my arm.

**Ronnie**   Don't make me then. (*He releases her.*)

**Pam**   You're violent. I don't know why your eyebrows aren't joined together. Like your moustache.

**Ronnie**   Shut up, will you. I've jumped a digit.

**Pam**   Remember the wedding? When Al put that underarm hair-remover on his eyebrows. So they didn't join together. For the wedding photos your best man looked like Henry Cooper. Eyes all swollen up and puffy. You did the milkman, didn't you?

**Ronnie**   Leave off, Pam. You're pissed.

**Pam**   I know you did him. You bastard. He was a nice man. Everyone here in the flats saying how terrible – and me knowing it was you, you bastard.

**Ronnie**   Don't get dramatic.

*She tops up her glass and goes to the coats.* **Ronnie** *checks his watch.*

Get a move on, Frank, get a move on.

**Pam**   Nice coat, real fur.

**Ronnie**   'Course it's real. No plastic smelling imitation stuff for these tight arsed nobs. Real pig stinking hide and leopard skin. And wardrobes smelling like fucking zoos. Here, try these for size.

**Pam**   What?

**Ronnie**   (*tosses them at her*)   Leather knickers.

**Pam**   Don't be disgusting, what do you take me for?

**Ronnie**   Go on!

**Pam**   Where did you get them?

**Ronnie**   (*produces whip and cracks it*)   Yeah!

**Pam**   (*screams and then laughs*)   God Almighty, how postively vile. How perverted.

**Ronnie**   Solicitor's house. In Tudor Avenue. Must be sixty grand. Right posh. There's a lot of fucking money about.

**Pam**  How perverted.

**Ronnie**  Leaded windows, carpets full of static. Get an electric shock everytime you touch a door handle. Bath like a Persian shit house. Perverts. Five grand here. We get nearer that apartment in Teneriffe.

**Pam**  The woman in the greengrocers said you can get a maid to keep the place clean during the out of season for seven quid a month. She said they're everso nice.

**Ronnie**  We'll have all that.

**Pam**  I'm everso surprised at the woman in the greengrocer's having one.

**Ronnie**  Show me anyone who's made a lot of money from nothing and I'll show you a villain.

**Pam**  I wonder if there's any Joy parfum in them presents? Go on, let me have a look.

*Enter* **Frank**; *suntanned man in an airline uniform.*

**Frank**  How are we going?

**Ronnie**  See for yourself.

**Frank**  Hello Pam. These yours? (*He fingers the leather knickers on the chair.*)

**Pam** (*giggling*)  Shall I try them on?

**Ronnie**  Pam!

**Pam**  You said –

**Ronnie**  Shut your hole! Good to see you Frank.

**Frank**  Happy Christmas.

**Ronnie**  It's a great night. Have a drink, Frank, have a drink. (*Hands him* **Pam**'s *glass.*)

**Frank**  Cheers.

**Ronnie**  Get the other addresses?

**Frank**  Got five. Here. There's a party on at Heathrow, so I'd better not hang about. Those addresses, all in this neighbourhood.

**Ronnie** (*looks at the list*)  Frank – take a colour tele, take a colour TV.

**Frank**  Another time. Be in touch.

**Frank** *goes and* **Ronnie** *continues to study the list.*

**Pam**  They're so dashing them airline pilots.

**Ronnie**  He's a fucking ticket clerk.

*Pause.* **Ronnie** *continues to read the list.* **Pam** *looks at presents.*

**Pam**  Don't you feel . . . (*Pause.*) Especially at Christmas?

**Ronnie**  What?

**Pam**  Doing it at Christmas?

*Pause.* **Ronnie** *lights a cigar slowly.*

**Ronnie**  Nothing. Feel, nothing.

**Pam**  All their houses? All twinkling with coloured lights and smelling nice and decorations?

**Ronnie**  No decorations for this lot. They'll all be in the fucking West Indies. Bastards spending Christmas in paradise. Good old Frank. These five families, be in the air time we detonate them.

**Pam**  (*reads list*)  Walnut Close, Raynor Hill. Such nice names, all with huge beautiful gardens I bet. Next Christmas I might be in our apartment in Teneriffe. And you in the Scrubs again.

**Ronnie** *slaps her face hard at the mention of prison. She tries to turn it into a joke.*

What if when we're in Teneriffe someone robs us?

**Ronnie**  Never . . . rob . . . your . . . own . . . class.

**Pam**  Robin Fucking Hood.

**Ronnie**  Tell Sid to come back here at about three in the morning. There'll be a second shipping. And tell him to lay off the booze till he's dropped it. (*Starts to go, stops.*) And if Smithy rings, ask him where the fuck he's been! (*He exits.*)

**Pam**, *alone, switches on the radio. Away in a Manger. Gingerly, she tries on the leather knickers, opening her dress to waist height to show them off. She sits and refills the glass.*

**Buddy** *enters quietly, wearing an old man's raincoat. He goes behind* **Pam** *and puts his hands over her eyes.*

**Pam** Buddy, Buddy – my darling little brother, it's you!

**Buddy** I waited till Ronnie went and then I come in.

**Pam** What are you doing here? And where did you get that thing? Just like that smelly old coat Uncle Harold used to wear.

**Buddy** Parole

*Pause.*

**Pam** Bit sudden in't it? No warning.

**Buddy** They was very generous, they said, well, seeing it's Christmas, all you that's on good behaviour, go home for a few days. (*He is staring at her leather knickers.*)

**Pam** O! A joke . . . (*Takes them off.*) Good to see you.

**Buddy** I went home, but there was no answer.

**Pam** Mum's in hospital again.

**Buddy** O, I wondered . . . when?

**Pam** Day before yesterday. No. It was Tuesday.

**Buddy** O.

**Pam** She'll be all right, just needs another transfusion.

**Buddy** They're getting more often.

**Pam** The doctor said that's what'd happen.

**Buddy** Ronnie's busy then.

**Pam** Yeah, one day I'll come in this room and be surprised because it's not full of fur coats and colour tellies.

**Buddy** Must have been planning this one. And him on probation and all.

**Pam** He can charm the leaves off the trees, my Ronnie can. She was here yesterday, his probation officer, daft cow. That post office job. Probation, his record! He sat on the stereo crying like a baby. Said it was all 'cause he saw his dad beat up his mum when he was a baby in his pram.

**Pam** *and* **Buddy** Vivid childhood memory!

**Pam** She believed him, lent him some Kleenex.

**Buddy** He's got a lucky one.

**Pam** No wonder he needs glasses to watch tv. (*Sees others.*) Teles. He says it himself, he does. It was reading all them fucking psychiatry books in the Scrubs. The bleeder. And they give you eighteen months for a few harmless little motors. There don't seem no justice. (*Pause.*) Take your coat off then. Might have given you something a bit more decent to wear in this weather. In't it bitter.

**Buddy** Bit nippy. Pam, ain't got an Anadin have you?

**Pam** Side of your face is all swelled up. Let me look, come here. Looks really painful.

**Buddy** Tooth hurting.

**Pam** Here, let me see. Turn round a bit.

*His coat falls open. She sees the uniform.*

**Pam** Buddy, them clothes! Buddy, Buddy, my darling little brother – they haven't let you out on parole. (*Pause.*) Don't lie to me. Enough lying in this family.

*Pause.*

**Buddy** I did a bunk, didn't I.

*Pause*

**Pam** Over the wall. On the run. With others? You was led astray . . .

**Buddy** Over the wall. On me own. (*Puts his hand over his head.*)

**Pam** But darling . . . why? You only had another four weeks. You said in your letter the governor had told you when you was leaving! In four weeks you'd have been out anyway.

**Buddy** I got . . .

*Pause.*

**Pam** What?

**Buddy** Fed up, bit fed up, you know. Frightened, Pam. Shaking, see? Can I have a fag?

**Pam** Yeah, here. (*Hands him a cigarette.*) I mean to say, my Ronnie's a bit highly strung and impetuous, but even he had the sense not to break out, not when you've only got a month to go.

**Buddy** And them Anadins?

**Pam** In me handbag.

**Buddy** *goes to the handbags on the truck.*

No, not that one. I haven't had a chance to go through all them yet. Looks really painful, way it's all swelling up.

**Buddy** It is.

*He takes two Anadins and swallows them, washing them down with* **Pam***'s whisky which makes him groan.*

**Pam** Then say, say it was the PAIN. Say you didn't know what you was doing because you was delirious with pain and . . . and . . .

**Buddy** Eh?

**Pam** Delirious with pain and could you please go back and would they please overlook it. Ronnie'll tell you what to say. Something psychiatric. Why you did it. Then he'll give you a lift back to the prison, after he's burgled the houses in Walnut Close and Tudor Drive.

**Buddy** Pam . . .

*Pause. He paces.*

**Pam** Weren't they waiting for you outside mum's?

**Buddy** Mum weren't there.

**Pam** She went into hospital.

**Buddy** Day before yesterday.

**Pam** Tuesday.

**Buddy** On Tuesday, yeah.

**Pam** For another –

**Buddy** Transfusion.

**Pam** – transfusion, you see the doctor said –

**Buddy** Killed this screw.

*He begins to shiver.*

**Pam** And the doctor said she'll have to have more transfusions more often now because the red corpuscles aren't reproducing so fast now that the –

**Buddy** This screw, I killed him.

**Pam** I thought that might have something to do with why we
can't have a baby, though I don't know how we'd get on in
Teneriffe with a baby, though mind you, we haven't got the
apartment yet and spending all these hundreds and hundreds of
pounds on tests and different treatments and then when we tried
to adopt, just on account of Ronnie's records the adoption
people said there's thousands of couples who are decent people
and can't have kids and so we couldn't even be considered. I
haven't got a criminal record.

**Buddy** I murdered this screw.

*Silence.*

**Pam** Buddy, Buddy, you mustn't murder screws, not screws.
That's not right.

**Buddy** Well, I did. So I run away.

*Pause*

**Pam** Is this a joke Buddy? A sick, sick joke to upset me?

**Buddy** Real. I can still hear the blood bubbling in his throat.

**Pam** Shouldn't have.

**Buddy** No.

**Pam** Shouldn't have.

**Buddy** I know.

**Pam** You was only in for stealing cars and now you've murdered a
screw. They'll . . . they'll kill you Buddy.

**Buddy** I went to Auntie Connie's.

**Pam** You should have hid there.

**Buddy** The police was there. I gave her a duck.

**Pam** A what?

**Buddy** A dead duck.

**Pam** I don't mind you killing ducks Buddy – but killing screws!
(*Pause.*) You're contaminated. (*She pours a larger whisky.*) Like they
say, there's nothing like money to attract money. Same with us.
Someone crooked in the family – and villainy is like the natural
course. For you. Just 'cause Ronnie had form, they kept their eye
out for you. And now you've made it worse.

**Buddy** Are you mad at me?

**Pam** No, not mad love. Just helpless. And tight round me belly. Like all the air's gone out of me lungs and they're squashed together. How did you get here?

**Buddy** Nicked a motor and dumped it.

**Pam** Nicked another one! Bad enough killing a screw without making it worse by nicking another car.

**Buddy** I had to.

**Pam** Didn't dump it here?

**Buddy** Dumped it at Mile End. Then got the tube.

**Pam** You didn't do it on purpose, did you Buddy?

**Buddy** It was an accident.

**Pam** Then go back and say you're sorry and it was an accident –

**Buddy** Pam, don't be stupid.

*Pause.*

**Pam** Ronnie'll know what to do for the best.

**Buddy** Pam, please don't keep getting drunk.

**Pam** Ronnie's in Walnut Close now. The posh houses in the big gardens. He's burgling them.

**Buddy** What house?

**Pam** The bloke from the airport wrote it down.

**Buddy** Airport?

**Pam** Heathrow. He gets the addresses from the flight reservations and gives them to Ronnie. Ronnie is smart. His brilliance – if he weren't bent he could be Prime Minister. (*Finds list.*) 14 Walnut Close . . . or is it 17?

**Buddy** I'll go there then.

**Pam** Yeah. (*Pours another drink.*) Don't get drunk you say. In this family?

**Buddy** Ronnie will help me, won't he? Got another fag?

**Pam** Take the packet.

**Buddy** Better then the prison baccy.

*He takes the cigarettes, kisses her briefly on the forehead and exits.* **Pam**
*stands and addresses the audience as back projection shows beautiful, rich
houses, dwelling on the Christmas decorations in their illuminated
windows. Spotlight on* **Pam**.

**Pam** Baccy and chocolate. That's all they think about inside.
When Ronnie goes down again, I'll leave him. I've had enough.
No house in Teneriffe, not really. And I'll get a get a man who
ain't got a record so that we can adopt a baby. They wouldn't let
us adopt because of Ronnie's record. I ain't got a record! But see
it's catching. Life of Riley for him. Nursery full of colour teles and
hiding the stolen jewellery in the kiddies' sandpit down there in
the yard. Full privileges on remand. When Ronnie came out last
time, he was all suntanned. And I'd lost a stone working in the
laundry. Baccy and chocolate, that's all they think about inside.
And how they'll slice up their wives if they so much as let another
bloke grope them. Let alone, you know. Life of Riley for Ronnie,
but not Buddy, no not Buddy if they find him. They will find him.
They'd found him before he'd even done anything. He was
already contaminated, because of Ronnie. Know what I mean? 14
Walnut Close must be such a nice house. Or is it 17? Funny
writing . . .

*Light fades on* **Pam** *and police radio messages about search for* **Buddy** *as
lights go up on* **Joan** *sitting on a stool writing Christmas cards and
talking on a wall telephone. A massive deep freeze behind her and
Christmas decorations. Police radio fades to Satie, and Satie fades after she
has begun speaking. She is in her early thirties, very Christian Dior.*

**Joan** Yes, Satie. I often feel like playing Satie. Not that I can play
Satie. Being unable to play the piano is a severe handicap. If you
can play the piano you are a much sought after guest. You are
always welcomed by people who have pianos. Especially by people
who have pianos and yet are unable to play them. I can play *Catch
a Falling Star* on one finger but I find that a good deal less than
rewarding. I love reading magazine articles about social
accomplishments. I read something fascinating in the
hairdressers about being a perfect guest and a perfect host. Yes,
um – how to hold a plate in one hand and a glass of chilled
Chablis in the other, while managing to to eat a chicken's leg
without getting your hands greasy. And what to do if whilst
holding a plate in one hand and a glass of chilled Chablis in the
other, your knicker elastic breaks and they slide down to your
ankles. Apparently it happens not infrequently. What you do is,
you calmly step out of them and place them in your handbag

while saying something so rivetting and extraordinarily fascinating that nobody notices. I spent days selecting an extraordinary thing to say in the event of such an emergency. I thought I'd say: 'Look behind the rose bushes. Isn't that the dustman fucking Princess Margaret?'

**Buddy** *enters, hesitates.*

The boy from the garage is here Edna. Toodaloo. (*Replaces phone receiver.*) I didn't hear you knock.

**Buddy** Wrong house, I wanted number 14, bye.

**Joan** This is number 14. Put it in the garage, did you?

**Buddy** Eh?

**Joan** The car?

**Buddy** Car.

**Joan** My car. Surely it's ready by now. Only a fault on the clutch, Mr Jameson said, though I'm sure he'll have charged me for a new gear box.

**Buddy** *hypnotised by the open deep freeze.*

**Buddy** All this food!

**Joan** I beg your pardon?

**Buddy** So much. All this, so much of it! What is this, a nosh shop?

**Joan** You are the carman, aren't you?

**Buddy** (*so amazed by the house, the deep freeze*) I've never been in a house like this, see.

**Joan** O . . . (*Smiles.*) I see. Not really imposing . . .

**Buddy** But impressive. (*Hand over head.*)

**Joan** Well perhaps. Are you unwell?

**Buddy** Bit . . . sick.

**Pam** There's a bug about.

**Buddy** I heard about it.

**Joan** You put my Fiesta in the garage, did you?

**Buddy** Yeah, yeah. So many nice things. Here. So much food.

**Joan** More economic. Inflation the way it is. Lambs are cheaper if you buy them whole.

**Buddy**  I couldn't agree more.

**Joan**  How much do I owe you?

**Buddy**  Owe me?

**Joan**  For the car?

**Buddy**  Yeah, yeah, right. Clutch, well . . . twenty-four quid. Say twenty-five, call it quits.

**Joan**  Is that all?

**Buddy**  O. Yeah, see, it weren't as bad as we thought. A leak in your clutch fluid canister and it got in the cable.

**Joan**  O don't destroy me with technical arguments.

**Buddy**  That's handy. I had better push off then lady. (*Anxious to go.*)

**Joan**  The bill?

**Buddy**  I forgot it. Dashing here to get your wheels back, like.

**Joan**  Wheels?

**Buddy**  What we in my trade call cars.

**Joan**  Wheels. How sweet.

**Joan**  Happy Christmas. (*Hands him six five pound notes.*) Half the Christmas box for you, half for Mr Jameson.

**Buddy**  Very decent of you.

**Joan**  I haven't seen you at the garage before, have I?

**Buddy**  Hidden out of the way, in case I frighten the punters, harr.

*Pause.* **Joan** *is very charming and a little flirting to him.*

**Joan**  O, don't forget the bill. For the dreaded VAT man. Curses!

**Buddy**  Curses!

**Joan**  Would you like a drink?

**Buddy**  Well, look . . . I think I'd better go lady.

**Joan**  Don't be shy.

**Buddy**  Nar . . .

**Joan**  O do have a drink. Christmas drinkies.

**Buddy**  Well –

**Joan**  A gin?

**Buddy**  Light ale please.

**Joan**  Yes, a gin it is. (*She begins to pour a very large one.*) Say *quand*.

**Buddy**  Beg your pardon?

**Joan**  Say 'when'.

**Buddy**  About half a gallon ago. Bit light headed . . . no food for . . .

**Joan**  There. (*Hands him glass.*)

**Buddy**  Cheers then. Help the flu. And me toothache.

**Joan**  You've got toothache?

**Buddy**  Yeah?

**Joan**  O, my husband's a dentist.

**Buddy**  Really? Great!

**Joan**  But he's away at a conference today.

**Buddy**  O . . .

**Joan**  And he's still waiting for the new Jaguar. And I was thinking . . . (*Seductive.*) The waiting list at your garage. I was wondering if there was some *periferique*, as it were, around it. Mmm?

**Buddy**  You what?

**Joan**  Some by-pass of the waiting list, if you know what I mean.

**Buddy**  You want a knocked-off Jag?

**Joan**  What?

**Buddy**  Sorry. Slip of the tongue.

**Joan**  Mister?

**Buddy**  Clark.

**Joan**  No relation to the Seymour-Clarks?

**Buddy**  Nar.

**Joan**  Mister Clark, we understand one another. I am prepared to pay above the list price for the first offer.

**Buddy** A Jag?

**Joan** When I brought the car in this morning, I.noticed that in your window there was a new model, exactly the colour my husband wants, in your showroom.

**Buddy** O yeah. Lovely colour.

**Joan** Lovely colour. And a sign on the window, it said: 'Sold.'

**Buddy** The waiting list, see.

**Joan** I am prepared to pay a little extra to get it.

**Buddy** Well, in this life you have to pay for what you fancy.

**Joan** I knew you'd understand.

**Buddy** How much?

**Joan** A hundred pounds?

**Buddy** (*amazed*) A hundred quid?

**Joan** (*thinking this inadequate*) A hundred and fifty?

**Buddy** (*quietly*) A hundred and fifty . . .

**Joan** We agree?

**Buddy** All right.

**Joan** And I take delivery?

**Buddy** All that.

**Joan** Tomorrow? You see, we're going to Paris for Christmas, to stay with friends and it would be so lovely to go in the new Jaguar.

**Buddy** Why not? If you've got the bread . . . (*Looks in deep freeze.*) So many many loaves in here.

**Joan** (*going to him at deep freeze*) Stocked up during the last baker's strike.

**Buddy** Don't miss a trick, do you, lady?

**Joan** (*hands him fifteen ten-pound notes*) Here, take it. I'll ring Mister Jameson in half an hour, so no tricks.

**Buddy** How could I compete with your tricks, lady? More bread in here than . . . (*Rummages inside deep freeze.*) Here, what's this?

**Joan**  Offals.

**Buddy**  Eh?

**Joan**  Brains. A delicacy, my husband loves them.

**Buddy**  Whose? Whose brain?

**Joan**  Pigs I think. Frozen. A delicacy.

**Buddy**  And this? (*Lifts a frozen eel.*)

**Joan**  Eels. Do you mind? Should there be any grease or oil on your hands . . . the hygiene risk . . .

**Buddy**  Contaminates them, eh?

*He twiddles with the frozen eel. Suddenly it is a weapon, a sword. He moves the pointed head to* **Joan**, *then presses it against her throat.*

**Buddy**  Interesting, what I'm saying, in't it? Very interesting. What is it?

**Joan**  Very interesting.

**Buddy**  Yeah. Hundred and fifty quid, eh? Just like that. Just like that! The car I nicked weren't even worth a hundred and fifty quid. 1970 Cortina. Clapped out heap of junk, not even worth a hundred and fifty. Not worth what you peel out like peanuts. Know what I got for it?

*Pause.* **Joan** *makes a dash for the telephone.* **Buddy** *pulls the lead out of the wall and threatens her with the sword again.*

I said: Do you know what I got for it? Guess.

**Joan**  Three hundred pounds?

**Buddy**  No. more, more. Don't play innocent.

**Joan**  I've no idea . . . what you're talking about. I don't know what you're doing or –

**Buddy**  I nicked a motor, right? Rusting shit, not the first I admit but . . . worth, value . . . one hundred and fifty greenuns. What did I get for it?

**Joan**  Five hundred pounds?

**Buddy**  See me hair? They take everything. Why take your hair and all. (*Scratches his short hair.*) They gave me eighteen months, lady. They locked me up, out of the way, in a prison for eighteen months.

**Joan**  So, you're not the mechanic at the garage?

**Buddy**  Ain't I seen you on Mastermind?

**Joan**  What do you want?

*Pause.*

**Buddy**  Dunno, lady. You're more a villain than me. Me brother-in-law, he says, says: 'Anyone with bread like this, they ain't got it legal.' I'm a villain . . .

*He sits on the deep freeze, shivers. He holds in one hand the screw's silver whistle. He dangles it on its chain, like a hypotist.*

Tooth on fire, lady. Needles in me head. On fire. (*Very slowly, now.*) I done the biggun. The biggun. (*Holds his head again.*) I done the murder. The one you used to have to swing for . . . Know what I mean? Nice here, nice. (*Jumps off the deep freeze.*) Tell me one thing? This really number 14?

**Joan**  Yes . . .

**Buddy**  Be glad you don't live at number 17, lady. Won't let you off with a frozen eel there tonight. (*Drops the eel, exits, blackout.*)

*During the blackout, another police radio message. In the blackout, we hear voices.*

**Ronnie**  All the lights out?

**Al**  Yeah. Can you hear him Ronnie?

**Ronnie**  He's round the back now. Coming this way. Hear him?

**Al**  I can fucking hear him.

**Ronnie**  Me heart's thumping like a piston engine.

**Al**  Fuck it, fuck it. Shall we make a run?

**Ronnie**  No Pandas out the front. No sign of the law or nothing.

**Al**  Sounds like . . . definitely only one of them. Bit light footed. Might be a fucking Japanese.

**Ronnie**  Japanese, what you talking about? Fucking Japanese?

**Al**  Or a Chinaman, they're small and all.

**Ronnie**  He's trying the French window.

*We become accustomed to the darkness. We see the frame of the French window upstage centre.*

**Al**  O Jesus. I thought you said they was in the West Indies?

**Ronnie**  Behind this curtain here. Soon as his head's in, let it go.

**Al**  Metal bar. Like the milkman. Parted his hair.

**Ronnie**  No fucking mistake .

*We see a shadowy figure trying the French windows from the outside.* **Al** *stands one side of window with a metal bar raised.* **Ronnie** *stands the other side. The window opens, enter a figure. Smash as the metal bar strikes the window frame.*

**Al**  Missed the cunt.

*Sound of* **Buddy** *falling, yelling.*

**Buddy**  Ronnie, Ronnie – leave off, it's only me.

**Ronnie**  You cunt.

*Lights on.* **Al** *wears a stocking over his head. A great pile of TV's, coats, jewellery etc. beside* **Ronnie** *who has just switched on the light.*

**Ronnie**  You stupid little bleeder. You daft bastard. You've made me piss me new trousers.

**Buddy**  Sorry.

**Ronnie**  I only fucking bought them yesterday.

**Al**  Who is he? (*He still stands holding the metal bar, blinking with surprise.*)

**Ronnie**  Pam's fucking brother. You nerk, you daft prat. What do you think you're doing?

**Buddy**  I come . . . to find you . . .

**Ronnie**  We're working, son, working! Big night tonight. Very big night.

**Al**  Ronnie, you've pissed your trousers.

**Ronnie**  Bleeding best ones ain't they.

**Al**  They look like your new ones.

**Ronnie**  They are me new ones! Might have had a bloody heart attack. Might have had.

**Ronnie** *kicks in the screen of a TV set.*

Now look what you've made me done.

**Al** Look what you've made Ronnie done.

**Ronnie** Me bloody nerves, like fuses popping all over me chest, you loon.

**Al** He's a bloody loon.

**Ronnie** He is.

**Al** I heard you say.

**Buddy** Ronnie . . . what do I do? (*Pause.*) Pam said, ask you – what to do.

**Ronnie** What are you talking about? I mean, what do you mean? Can't you see, you flat-footed ponce –

**Al** Oi. I've got flat feet. (*Takes the stocking off his head.*)

**Ronnie** No offence, .

**Al** If I hadn't got flat feet, I'd have been a copper.

**Ronnie** I'm talking about him.

**Al** Bloody flat-footed ponce.

**Ronnie** A lot of organising has gone into this night, Buddy. A lot of very detailed planning involving a lot of very talented people and you have just strolled in right nonchalant and stuffed a fucking candelabra up me arsehole. (*Kicks in another TV screen.*) , you should have splattered his skull.

**Buddy** I broke out.

**Ronnie** Eh, what?

**Buddy** Broke out, over the wall, on the run. And . . . this screw got killed.

Buddy *holds his head again. Pause.*

It was an accident.

**Ronnie** Listen . . . you kidding me?

**Buddy** Accident. Really.

**Ronnie** Screw dead?

**Al** A screw. Bleeding bloody Buddha. Prat.

**Ronnie** You knocked off a fucking screw? My God! There'll be Concordes crashing on your head, boy. That is not done, that is not right, that is too much.

**Al**  Bleeding bloody Buddha, you prat!

**Buddy**  Please Ronnie, do something. Help me.

**Ronnie**  Help you? Help you? God Almighty and all his angels cannot help you, kiddo. You have done what is never done. No-one murders screws.

**Al**  A bloke in Parkhurst murdered a screw once.

**Ronnie**  I'm talking about him.

**Al**  Mind you, it was the first time he'd been abroad.

**Buddy**  Didn't mean it. I've got toothache.

**Ronnie**  (*heavy sarcasm*)  O, he had toothache! Poor little sod. Nothing wrong with knocking off a screw if you've got toothache.

**Buddy**  (*clings to him*)  Please Ronnie, I've been everywhere else.

**Ronnie**  If anyone saw you come here . . . Fucking idiot. (*Throws* **Buddy** *off.*)

**Al**  Idiot. Come on, better split.

**Ronnie**  Two grand here, two grand. Two fucking Gs boy. That's what you've smashed up.

**Al**  I'll get the motor.

**Al** *exits.* **Ronnie** *breathes furiously and tears up a fur coat. Stands panting, kicks jewellery.*

**Ronnie**  Do you know what you have done? With your obscene perverted presence here? You have blown months of planning, of chatting up the geezer from Heathrow with double scotches like there's no tomorrow. You have fucked it all up! Kaboosh, kaputt. Old Bill'll be round our flat like greased fucking lightning now.

**Buddy**  When I broke out, I didn't know you had a big night on.

**Ronnie**  Should I have sent you a telegram? First thing they'll do, right? Be round your mum's. Then round Pam's. You cunt. The flat's full of gear! I just hope Sid's picked it up by now. I'll have to dump the jewellery in the kid's sand-pit outside.

**Buddy**  I didn't know!

**Ronnie**  Why didn't you just keep away? You're on your own. Law of decency that. Villains' code. Do not contaminate others with what you have done when what you have done is disgusting even by villains' code. Scum.

**Ronnie**  Ronnie, please.

**Al** *enters. Sound of revving car off.*

**Al**  We'd better leave all this and get away. Fast.

**Ronnie**  Yeah, and warn Frank at Heathrow before the law starts sniffing the snot up his nostrils. (*To* **Buddy**.) If I go down again because of you, you leading them onto me . . . (*Pause.*) I'll fucking slice you. And that's promise. Comprendi?

**Buddy**  Sorry.

**Ronnie**  You will be. (*He puts on long leather overcoat*)

**Al**  Come on.

**Ronnie** (*to* **Al**)  He'll be sorry.

**Al**  He will be sorry.

**Buddy**  What shall I do?

**Ronnie**  Dig a grave. (*Exits.*)

**Al**  Yeah, dig a grave. For yourself.

**Ronnie** *and* **Al** *exit through the French windows.* **Buddy** *watches them go, then takes off his raincoat and selects a fur-hooded anorak and puts that on, transferring cigarettes etc. from pockets. He dwells, holding the screw's silver whistle.*

*Sound of* Silent Night *off. He freezes, then relief when he realises it's carol singers. They knock on front door, still singing.* **Buddy** *exits through the French windows, switching off the light.*

*The carol continues in the blackout, then lights on a hospital bed. A blood drip.*

*A* **Priest** *in vestments stands at the foot of the bed. The carol continues. There are three candles lit on the bed table.*

**Priest**  God the father of mercies/Through the death and resurrection of His Son/Has reconciled the world to himself/And sent the Holy Spirit among us/For the forgiveness of sins;/Through the Ministry of the Church/May God give your pardon and peace/And I absolve you from your sins/In the name of the Father and of the Son and of the Holy Spirit, Amen.

**Buddy** *has entered holding a candle.*

**Buddy** Amen.

The **Priest** *looks at* **Buddy**.
**Buddy** *sets the candle on the table.*

**Buddy** Hello. How is she?

**Priest** Are you a relative?

**Buddy** She's me mum

**Priest** Your mother?

**Buddy** I'm her son.

**Priest** You're Buddy?

**Buddy** Yeah. She don't arf look ill.

**Priest** She's had a considerable transfusion. You always look like that after a transfusion.

**Buddy** Me sister, she don't reckon she's at all well. Do you come to everyone here?

**Priest** Yes, I do.

**Buddy** You don't just come to people who are . . . you know?

**Priest** No. She is . . . very poorly.

**Buddy** Your choir? Sounds nice. None of them in football boots.

**Priest** The choir?

**Buddy** At me sister's wedding, noticed the choir, when they pushed off at the end, under their dresses –

**Priest** Cassocks.

**Buddy** Yeah. They was wearing football boots. Dashing off to a match.

**Priest** Your mother, Buddy –

**Buddy** She don't look at all well.

**Priest** She told me you were in Borstal.

*Pause.*

**Buddy** I was.

**Priest** You've finished there?

**Buddy** Ah. Look, what are you doing now?

**Priest** Going home for my tea.

**Buddy** I wonder if I could have a word with you?

**Priest** By all means.

*Pause.*

You say, you've just left Borstal? When did you leave?

**Buddy** Not long ago.

**Priest** What do you want to tell me?

**Buddy** Um, see . . . people will think I've committed a sin.

**Priest** Yes?

**Buddy** When I say I've left Borstal . . . the thing is, they don't know I've left.

**Priest** I see.

**Buddy** I thought perhaps you could go and have a word with them. Like, when you get a bit panicky – see, I got a bit panicky – when you're panicky, you don't know what to do.

**Priest** Am I to understand that you've absconded . . . I mean, run away?

**Buddy** Absconded, yeah.

**Priest** Why did you? Your mother was very happy that you were going to be released after Christmas.

**Buddy** She don't look too happy now, does she? You see . . . there was this accident and I got worried.

**Priest** What sort of accident? To make you leave?

**Buddy** O Christ! Sorry . . . you see . . . ah . . . um . . .

**Priest** Take your time, explain in your own words. You had an accident?

**Buddy** I didn't. He did. Did you see the film *Soldier Blue*?

**Priest** No.

**Buddy** Pity. See, they was playing football and when the ball went over the wall, I had to get it and it was on the river, on the ice, and I found this dead duck and I got this plank to get the ball because

I couldn't reach and this Henderson –

**Priest**  Another boy?

**Buddy**  Nar, a screw –

**Priest**  A warder?

**Buddy**  Yeah, he come out to see what I was doing and we had this chat about this duck because he likes ducks – well, he used to and . . . there was this accident.

*Pause.*

**Priest**  Is that all?

**Buddy**  I've got toothache. And he was nice to me. He was going to get a dentist and I was getting the plank and I turned round and hit him with the plank and, this is ridiculous (*Giggles.*) It's funny. But it ain't 'cause, the plank hit him and the spike went in him and . . . I thought he was joking. And . . .

*Pause.*

**Buddy**  He was dead. And I run. I've been all over the place and I reckoned you could have a word with them and explain it was an accident.

**Priest**  Was it an accident?

**Buddy**  'Course it was an accident.

**Priest**  You didn't mean to kill him?

**Buddy**  I didn't kill him! He just died. I swear, I swear on me mum's life . . . I know they won't believe it. Do you believe it?

**Priest**  I want to know . . . more about it.

**Buddy**  It sounds stupid.

**Priest**  It sounds a little unlikely.

**Buddy**  Yeah.

**Priest**  Do you have a record of violence?

**Buddy**  TDA . . . Taking and driving away . . . nicking cars, that's all. She looks terrible.

**Priest**  She's –

**Buddy**  They'll murder me.

**Priest**  Why do you think the authorities will disbelieve you?

**Buddy**  They don't trust no-one.

**Priest**  But surely that's part of their jobs, as policemen.

**Buddy**  Look, do you believe me? That it was an accident?

**Priest**  Yes, I do.

**Buddy**  (*amazed*)  Why?

**Priest**  I believe you because, the utter idiocy of it all. That, I think, is in your favour (*Looks at his watch.*)

**Buddy**  You in a hurry?

**Priest**  No.

**Buddy**  Good, 'cause what I want you to do for me – will you do it for me, won't you? – what I'd like you to do is, go there to the Borstal and . . . tell them it was an accident. For me.

**Priest**  Wouldn't it be better if you came with me to corroborate what you want me to say?

**Buddy**  They'll think, if I'm there, they won't believe me.

**Priest**  Assuming it was, as you say, an accident . . . are you firm in your decision not to go back?

**Buddy**  I'd explain to them, but they won't listen.

**Priest**  It'll be difficult for me to persuade them, to convince them that it was an accident.

**Buddy**  You've got a better chance than I have.

**Priest**  So, if I go to the governor and explain, plead your case, your side . . . where will you stay? Your mother's flat? (*Pause.*) Shall I find a place for you to stay?

**Buddy**  Do you mean that?

**Priest**  I do. But you will have to go back there eventually. You're afraid of the consequences of being charged with a murder?

**Buddy**  Don't say that!!!

**Priest**  A killing. I can't promise you any results. You must trust me.

**Buddy**  How can I trust that you believe me?

**Priest**  It's bizarre enough to be the truth. I shall tell them that it was an accident and do my best to ensure that the authorities are unbiased when . . . you face them.

**Buddy** You'll go now then?

**Priest** Let us pause a moment and . . . quietly pray.

*Pause. The* **Priest** *stands in silent prayer.* **Buddy** *takes the money* **Joan** *had given him from his pocket and puts it on the bed near the* **Priest**. *He is nervous at the inactivity. Suddenly the bell sounds.* **Buddy** *panics and dashes off. The* **Priest** *calls after him:*

**Priest** Buddy, Buddy – that was only the bell for the end of visiting. Buddy.

*The* **Priest** *begins to run after him as Blackout. Music loud: latest top single hit, very loud. Then flashing coloured lights of an amusement arcade and* **Buddy** *with a one-armed bandit, stage centre. He speaks directly to the audience as pop songs continue quietly in the background:*

**Buddy** Fuck me, dishing out the vicar a hundred and fifty quid and me without a penny in me pocket. (*Takes a beer can tag from his pocket and spits on it.*) These Southend blokes in there, they told me how to do it. They made a fortune on the bandits with a beer can tag and the juice. What you need is a little squirt of the old three in one motor oil. Three in one motor oil, like you use in the carbs, know what I mean? Jams the machine. Fucks the mechanism. Trade secret, I'm telling you. (*Laughs.*) Put the tag in . . . (*Puts the tag in the coin slot. Bangs the machine, shakes it.*) Count ten, give the oil time to ooze the motor . . . one, two, three, four, five, six, seven, eight, nine, ten and . . . Jackpot!

*Hundreds of coins pour out.* **Buddy** *kneels to collect them. Enter* **Dave** , *same age, with crash helmet.*

**Dave** Oi . . .

**Buddy** (*leaps up, shocked*) Fucking hell . . .

**Dave** (*very nervous*) Christ, are you up to here in it.

**Buddy** Thanks for coming Dave.

**Dave** You shouldn't have phoned me. Shouldn't have.

**Buddy** You give me your number.

**Dave** For when you was out legit. Not . . . I'm straight now, straight, ain't I? Don't want to go back there.

**Buddy** Thanks for coming.

**Dave** Here.

**Buddy** You got it?

**Dave** Me sister got it, from the chemists.

**Buddy** I remember you said she works in a chemists. Tar.

**Dave** It's an emergency filling. It's kinda like chewing gum, see. Heat it up in hot water and then stick it in your tooth and . . . Christ. The size of your face.

**Buddy** (*pockets the emergency filling*) Thanks Dave.

**Dave** I shouldn't be here. If the law found me here with you . . . Christ! Which one was it?

**Buddy** Henderson.

**Dave** The Donald Duck bloke?

**Buddy** Yeah. (*Behaves a little nonchalantly because of* **Dave** *'s awe*).

**Dave** He was a nice bloke, not like the others, Why him?

**Buddy** It was an accident.

**Dave** In the chest. Jesus Buddy – ain't like you.

**Buddy** I was standing outside to get the ball and . . . match with the village team –

**Dave** Who won?

**Buddy** We was winning three-one. Jamie scored two.

**Dave** Jamie's a cart-horse. Always beat the village poufs. Nicking the machines . . . it works then. What the Southend blokes said.

**Buddy** *pockets the remainder of the coins.*

**Buddy** They all got a year. Woman tonight, posh woman – she gave me a hundred and fifty quid to jump the queue for her for a new Jag.

**Dave** You're joking!

**Buddy** A hundred and fifty quid in tenners. What I nicked weren't worth that.

**Dave** Well, that's not the point, is it?

**Buddy** Why ain't it (*Pause.*) Why ain't it?

**Dave** (*laughs unsurely*) You and your questions! Giggles with the trick cyclist. Why why why . . .

**Buddy**  He couldn't answer them. Can you?

**Dave**  For fuck's sake, Buddy, I went out on a limb to bring the thing for your tooth. I'm going.

**Buddy**  (*shouts, pleads*)  Someone's gotta help me!

**Dave**  Your mum –

**Buddy**  She's in hospital again –

**Dave**  Sorry. (*Jittery.*)  Look, I've gotta go now. Say the Old Bill clock me here, accomplice or something . . .

**Buddy**  Why did they keep picking on me?

**Dave**  They're fucking entitled to now, after what you've done.

**Buddy**  What?

**Dave**  Murdering a screw.

*Pause. It sinks in. Just the pop song and the flashing coloured lights.*

**Buddy**  Say that again.

**Dave**  Eh?

**Buddy**  Say me name and then . . . say what I've done.

**Dave**  How do you mean?

**Buddy**  I . . . I . . . (*Pause.*)  I can't believe it, see.

**Dave**  Buddy . . .

**Buddy**  Yeah?

**Dave**  Buddy, on the news on the telly . . . I was having me tea . . . there was this photo of you and they said, Kenneth Kendall said: police wished to interview you to help them with their inquiries following the murder of a screw at the Borstal. You, they said. There was this photo, of you.

*Pause.*

**Buddy**  I'm only 17.

**Dave**  They never said that. You had long hair in the photo.

**Buddy**  They take everything. Why take your hair and all? They'll find me soon.

**Dave** They always do. Look, what you want to do is . . .

*Pause.*

**Buddy** What?

**Dave** Go somewhere, to someone, like . . . who you can trust. Who'll hide you and protect you so they won't rough you up. Someone who'll . . .

*Pause.*

**Buddy** Like who?

**Dave** There must be *someone.*

**Buddy** Yeah there must be. Ain't Ronnie, though. Ain't Pam, ain't me mum, ain't the priest, ain't Auntie Connie and ain't Uncle Harold. He's dead. And ain't the posh woman – what she does, more wrong than what I done.

**Dave** I am going now.

**Buddy** All right. Tar Dave.

**Dave** How did the spuds I planted come up?

**Buddy** Really nice. Dug 'em up for Christmas dinner. Dave . . .

**Dave** What?

**Buddy** Did it ever seem to you, like . . . when you was in there . . . you know some of them . . . their faces, their eyes . . . you knew they was going to be in there, or another prison, always be there, all their lives . . . Did it seem like that to you? Like, it'd be the place you was always gonna be?

*Pause.*

**Dave** Better be going. So cold, looks like it'll snow tonight.

**Buddy** Can I come and stay the night at your flat?

**Dave** For Christ's sake Buddy. Don't ask me that. 'Course you can't. I'm a reformed person now. Gonna get a job.

**Buddy** Ain't you had one?

**Dave** Not since I was released. There's a helluva shortage. But then, I ain't got into no more trouble neither.

**Buddy** Thank your sister for me.

**Dave** *nods and goes.*

*Cut music. Blackout, but: Spotlight on* **Buddy** *fingering the whistle.*

**Buddy** (*to the audience*)  There was this madman in the park. Years ago, scared away the kids. Ran past him. He only had one leg. The other one was wooden. Then one winter, it snowed a lot . . .

*Snowflakes begin to fall. Dim lights on empty stage. The back projection is of a deserted dockside at night.*

And the madman disappeared. And when the weather warmed up and the snow melted they found his body in the pond in the park. And when all the snow had gone, they found his wooden leg and on it he had carved: 'Goodbye cruel world.'

*Voice off singing First World War song* 'Good-byee'.

*A tractor tyre on a rope is lowered – an impromptu swing.*

**Buddy** *swings on it. There is a snow covered sand-pit stage centre.*

*The singing gets nearer.*

**Voice**  Shut up.

**Voice 2**  The kids in here are trying to get to sleep.

**Voice 3**  I'll come down there and lay you out, you dirty, smelling, child-molesting cunt.

*Enter* **Sammy**, *in tramp clothes – old army uniform. He finishes the song.* **Buddy** *laughs. Snow falls more heavily.*

**Sammy**  Snowing.

**Buddy**  Yeah.

**Sammy**  Can you lend me a bob or two?

**Buddy**  Help yourself.

**Buddy** *tosses a handful of bandit coins onto the snow of the kid's sandpit.*

**Sammy**  Thank you, thank you. But it would have been a hell of a lot easier if you'd . . .

*He gets on his knees to pick them up.*

There's sand underneath here.

**Buddy**  Sand-pit for the kids in the flats.

**Sammy**  So high, all around. So many towers. You live here?

**Buddy**  Sort of. On and off.

**Sammy** I have not a home myself.

**Buddy** I figured that.

**Sammy** I move around. Have to get pissed tonight, I will. Then I'll be warm.

**Buddy** How's that?

**Sammy** Find me in the gutter, lock me up. The police will. Bed and breakfast. That's home. When it's too cold to be out on the streets. Ice at night.

**Buddy** Yeah.

**Sammy** Your face is swollen – been fighting?

**Buddy** Nar.

**Sammy** I was a fighter. Fighting – it's the highest and honourablest action for any man. You must fight boy. Eyes full of fear. Searching eyes. You in trouble boy?

**Buddy** You could say that.

**Sammy** *beats his hands with cold, puts them under his armpits.*

**Sammy** Never as bad as it seems. Never.

**Buddy** *laughs, swings higher.*

**Sammy** Don't laugh at me, don't laugh at me, boy. Old tramp, that right? Old nothing in his ragged clothes, shit under his finger-nails. Fighter boy, me. Fighter. I could biff. I could wallop. Don't be frightened of me. See your eyes. See, you know. Prison face. Whatever you've done – Old eyes in a child's face. No innocence there. What you done, boy?

**Buddy** *swings, turning his back on* **Sammy***. Snow is falling still more heavily.*

**Sammy** When I'm pissed they give me bread and breakfast in the nick. Blood and snot, that was me. I was a boxer, boy. Sammy the name.

*He drinks from a beer bottle, then hands it to* **Buddy***.*

**Buddy** Me father, he was a boxer too. Died in the Barking Canal. Got pissed, fell in then come to the surface ten times and drowned. He was waiting for the count of eight (*Laughs.*) I had four fights a week. When the weather was good, followed the summer fairs. When winter come, the cities. Booths in the fairgrounds at the end, with the freak shows. Some nights, as the snow fell, hands so numb with the cold I could hardly make a fist. I got me title. One night, I got me title. The finest fighter in the land. Piss me trousers now. Shamed meself last time I was in the dock of the court. I shitted. Lost control of me bowels, see. Coppers had to mop it up. Sneered at me, laughed at me, turned up their noses. 'All right,' I says. 'Who do you think you're snotting at? Do what you like to me, take away from me what you like. One thing you can never do. You can never take away the day I won me title.' Whatever becomes of me, they can never take away the night I won me title.

**Buddy** Whatever becomes of me . . . never take away the day I spiked a screw.

*Pause.* **Buddy** *stops swinging.*

**Sammy** There's a man who helps boys in trouble. Albert. Albert his name, they call him Lord Plaistow now. I been to him. I've had troubles. Trust him. Fine man. Times no-one'll help, Albert, Lord Plaistow, he'll help. Tell you where he lives, give you his phone number. Always phone him up, in trouble. Here.

*Hands* **Buddy** *a paper from his tobacco tin.*

Say Sammy sent you, Sammy who one night was British lightweight champion.

**Buddy** *gets off the swing, pockets the address.*

**Sammy** You'll need money for the phone, money for the fare.

**Sammy** *hands* **Buddy** *some coins.* **Buddy** *nods, then exits.*

**Sammy** Never take away the night I won . . . Never take away the day he . . .

*Kneels and buries his hands in the sand-pit.*

Good God! There's necklaces in the sand.

*Holds up necklaces and rings.*

And watches and rings and jewellery and . . . God thank you. For such a reward for one little act of kindness.

*He laughs.*

*Blackout.*

*Music: John Lennon's* 'So This is Christmas' *from the album* Shaved Fish.

# Act Two

*Music before act: Lennon's 'So This Is Christmas'.*

*Lights up on an elegant room full of Christmas decorations; a tree, presents etc. The table is laid for a dinner party. **Edna**, about 50, and dressed very elegantly, enters, and addresses the audience as the music fades. She wears a brightly-coloured paper Christmas party hat.*

**Edna** Guests will be arriving by the minute. A dinner party to celebrate the Christmas recess. Henry's cooking. He loves to cook. And I must switch on the fairy lights.

*She switches on twinkling tree lights.*

Fairy lights create such a warm ambience. And hide my wrinkles. They are especially plentiful around my neck, which is why I wear so many pearls. And music! Guitar concerto.

*Guitar concerto on hi-fi. Rodrigues.*

Love this. Reminds me of our holidays in Spain. Granada, Marbella, Lorett, Salami.

**Henry's Voice** No salami tonight Edna. Ha ha.

**Edna** Need a hand darling?

**Henry's Voice** No thanks, Edna. Wait till you taste this paté. Yum yum.

**Edna** Henry is so tired since he's been a Minister. A junior minister. He works so hard with the awful business of government and his directorships. We don't fuck much now, except on the occasional fact-finding tours. When we were young we fucked a lot. At Oxford – Henry was at the university and I lived in a village outside. I lived for ponies until Henry swept me off my feet as though on some invisible great white charger. Daddy was fearfully upset when he heard Henry was a Socialist. But as I said to mummy, he *had* to be Labour or he might never have got a seat.

*Enter **Henry** in a Pears Soap advert apron and with a plate of paté. He too wears a party hat. He has an occasional stutter.*

**Henry** Paté! Ex . . . ex . . . ex . . . .

**Edna** Excellent? Extraordinary?

**Henry** Exquisite. Sucking pig. A real sucking pig would have been too ostentatious but paté – sucking pig.

*He exits having deposited the paté on the table.*

**Edna**  I refuse to perform fellatio. I'm on a low calorie diet and I'm concerned at the calories intake of the . . . thingy. Besides, the home and the children are my life. Fiona and Sarah are sweet, but I'm awfully worried at the set Adam has got himself into. At Harrow. I was alarmed when he came to the golf club wearing a safety pin in his nose. Henry wants him to read Greats at Oxford, but it's most distressing, this punk thing. I mean, when he was here at Easter, things kept appearing in his bedroom and the harness for Fiona's pony disappeared. He's gone to see the Boomtown Rats at the Rainbow tonight.

**Henry**  (*entering with a glass*)  He jolly well ought to get his head down and get on with his w . . . w . . . work.

**Edna**  Exactly.

**Henry**  Garlic. (*Shows a bottle of pickled garlicks, sniffs them.*)

**Edna**  Henry, really! I insist.

**Henry**  It is essential to the dish I am preparing.

**Edna**  We cannot inflict garlic on our guests.

**Henry**  Edna, you and I have had this f . . . f . . . friction before –

**Edna**  I'd have preferred something more traditional anyway. A roast.

**Henry**  The garlic is essential. In the *Evening Standard*, Delia Smith says pickle it, thereby ensuring that the qualities of the garlic that in you arouse such h . . . h . . . hostility are reduced by the process of pickling. It isn't like garlic.

**Edna**  Then what is the point of having it?

**Henry**  Because it is correct. For centuries the French have used the garlic in this dish to bring out the flavour and I really object to . . . Look. It's a perfect compromise. Garlic that doesn't taste like garlic.

**Edna**  I wish you'd take as much trouble with the Brussel sprouts.

**Henry**  I am. (*Smells.*) Ah, tomatoes provencal. Wonderful tip old Delia – growing them in the drain.

**Edna**  Please be sure not to say anything like that to Joan, not tonight. Poor Joan.

**Henry**  She's been up there an awful long time.

**Edna**  And Peter still not back from the conference.

**Henry**  I just hope Albert behaves himself.

**Edna**  You could have ensured his punctual presence by escorting him back from the bar.

**Henry**  He wasn't there. He was doing his Santa Claus thingy, at Great Ormond Street.

*Cooker bell pings off.*

Ah time to heat the Espagnol sauce. (*Exits.*

**Edna** (*loud*)  I saw the temperatures of the West Indies in *The Times*. I think this will be the most enjoyable winter holiday –

**Henry's Voice** (*off*)  Business trip. Work, darling, work. We really must get some renegotiations under way for their poor sugar industry. That EEC deal was appalling.

**Joan** *enters, beautifully dressed, but melancholic.*

**Edna**  Darling! Feeling better now?

**Joan**  I just can't get over the shock.

**Edna**  Of course. It must have been a frightful shock.

**Joan**  It was absolutely appalling. To have been held up at knife point –

**Henry** *enters with a glass and a sherry bottle.*

**Henry**  More, I thought, eel tail.

**Edna**  Be quiet Henry.

**Joan**  I suppose I was lucky, being in, I mean. Two other houses in the road were ransacked. Everything stolen, the police said. And the wilful destruction of property. And the poor Woods, those clocks. They . . . they just excreted in their bed.

**Henry**  I expect it was the shock at discovering the break-in.

**Edna**  Henry!

**Joan**  I meant, the burglars.

**Henry**  Ah. Need the sherry for the old . . . (*Exits with the sherry bottle.*)

*The telephone rings as* **Joan** *sits.*

**Edna**  That'll be Albert I expect. I'm glad Lord Plaistow is coming
– livens us all up.

**Joan**  He always makes me laugh, he's so amusing.

**Edna**  Henry says he hasn't quite been himself since they put him
in the Lords. Making Albert a Lord, the thought of it! (*Speaking on
the phone.*) Albert darling. What? O no. But I mean, it's Christmas!
Well, can't you see him quickly and come? O do. Joan and Peter'll
be here and . . . you really can't let us down. Please. (*Replaces the
receiver.*) Henry. Albert on the phone. He said he might not be
able to come.

*Enter* **Henry.**

**Henry**  What?

**Edna**  He's had a panic phone call from some youngster from his
old constituency . . . So he's staying at home to see him.

**Henry**  That's q . . . q . . . quintessential Albert.

**Edna**  At Christmas though?

**Henry**  I do admire Albert in a way. All his stuff with kids. I'm
pretty sure the emotional involvement is a mistake but –

**Edna**  (*sudden inspiration*)  Why don't we . . .

**Henry**  What?

**Edna**  Why don't we ask Albert to bring the youngster here?
Albert and his waifs and strays, he's always helping people in
trouble, especially kids. Like his Santa Claus thingy this
afternoon. He does so much that's good but never reaches the
papers.

**Henry**  By all accounts Crossman was asleep half the time.

**Edna**  Let's ask him to bring the youngster here. I insist Henry.
Lots of our friends take orphans in at Christmas. From Barnados
and what have you. All I'm asking is, we ask Albert to bring the
little stranger here so that we can give him a jolly decent
Christmas and a nice meal.

**Henry**  Edna, for goodness sake, the one thing that can be said for
the Welfare State for all its loopholes and shortcomings is that not
many go short of a decent meal at Christmas.

**Edna** O Henry, do say yes. We have so much to share. Far more than we actually need. And it would be lovely – a real old fashioned family Christmas. It isn't really the same in the West Indies. This is our only chance tonight before we go. To share a family Christmas with a deprived youngster. I could get some of Adam's toys out of the attic and wrap them up as presents and . . . it'll be just like Christmas was when our children were young. Do agree.

**Henry** Joan, tell her she's being ridiculous.

**Joan** I'm not sure that she is. I know what she means about wanting to share. To share our good fortune with someone less fortunate than ourselves. We seriously thought about a child from one of the council homes. We might have done it if we hadn't been going to France.

**Henry** Look Edna, what do you suppose might be the effect on the child afterwards – after being subjected to a bellyful of liberal, middle-class do-gooding?

**Edna** You're so cynical. You weren't like this when I married you. You were terribly Socialist.

**Henry** I've been a professional Socialist for 20 years now Edna and –

**Joan** I don't think of you as a Socialist Henry. You're a Minister.

**Henry** Look, I want to make my position on this absolutely clear.

**Edna** Whenever you say that, it's a euphemism for you haven't an idea in your head.

**Henry** Quite the contrary actually. The producer of *Any Questions* congratulated me on the breadth of subjects upon which I did have opinions. I was the only member of the panel who spoke as long about nappy rash as the prospect of a lasting peace formula in the Middle East.

**Edna** That's because you stutter every time you say an Arab name.

**Henry** S . . . S . . . S

**Edna** Sadat?

**Henry** Sod off. (*Exits.*)

**Edna** You do think it's a good idea, don't you Joan?

**Joan** Yes.

**Edna**  I shall phone Albert. The good Lord Plaistow . . .

*Lights off* **Edna** *'s room. Telephone ringing. Lights up on sofa of* **Albert** *'s room. He enters with a bottle and glass singing; he wears a Santa Claus costume. There is a sack of presents beside the sofa.*

**Albert**  When I'm leaning on the lampost at the corner of the street
Waiting for a certain laddie to pass by,
O me, O my,
Waiting for a laddie to pass by.

*Answers phone. He is a little drunk.*

Hello, Lord Plaistow speaking. Edna who? Madam, I assure you I have never heard of anyone called Edna. Ah . . . of course it was a joke, Edna, dear dear Edna. Just a bit of festive Yuletide bonhomie. O wonderful, wonderful. Seemed to have cheered the kiddies up this afternoon. I find I only have to mention Harold's last Honours List and even children laugh. Bloody disc-jockey they had there got all the attention. No-one had ever heard of me. What, the waif and stray coming here? Jolly decent of you Edna, jolly decent of you. Old friend told him to phone me so I feel a certain sense of . . . duty would be the wrong word, but I'm damned if I can think of the right one.

*Doorbell rings off.*

Ah, that must be my little stranger. OK Edna, we shall see, we shall see. I'll be along in half an hour anyway. We'll see about this kiddie.

*Replaces telephone. On intercom:*

Fine lad, fine. Door opening now. Be sure to give it a bit of a bang from behind. I'm second on the left past the lift.

*Replaces intercom receiver, continues to sing and dance as he pours drink and sits.* **Buddy** *enters, shivering.* **Albert** *stops singing.*

**Albert**  George Formby.

**Buddy**  Lord Plaistow?

**Albert**  Yes. George Formby's dead.

**Buddy**  I didn't know that.

**Albert**  Did you know Marc Bolan's dead?

**Buddy**  Eh?

**Albert**  I never knew he was alive.

**Buddy**  He was a singer. T Rex group.

**Albert**  Little girlie at Great Ormond Street this afternoon – fearfully upset the DJ didn't have a Marc Bolan record. All these singers dropping off: Callas, Bing, Elvis. If I'd known about Bolan as well I'd have probably stopped singing in my bath. Irresistible temptation for fate.

**Buddy**  Me mum liked Buddy Holly – that's why she called me Buddy.

**Albert**  Singer eh? Good job she wasn't wild about the Great Carouso. Never mind, never mind. You're shivering?

**Buddy**  Getting colder. Real ice out.

**Albert**  Warm yourself in front of the fire here.

**Buddy**  Real brass monkey.

**Albert**  Can't be that bad or they would have cancelled the match tonight. Hammers are still playing.

**Buddy**  O.

**Albert**  Sit down lad, a sit down. Make yourself at home. Drink? (*Pours a large whisky and gives it to* **Buddy**.) So old Sammy told you to seek me out.

**Buddy**  The old boxer.

**Albert**  How do you know him?

**Buddy**  I met him.

**Albert**  One night he was champion of the British Empire. Hands up, arms outstretched beneath the arc lights with a golden belt clipped around his waist. Two years later – in the gutter. Couple of fights after his championship, he killed a man in the ring. O, his opponent shouldn't have been there in the first place, some head injury. But the laws were more lax then, the medical examinations less thorough. But old Sammy was prohibited from ever putting on professional gloves again – not that he ever wanted to. The death wreaked havoc on Sammy's life. I like Sammy. Spent more nights in the nick than out. I only see him when he's in trouble. About time I heard from him again. (*Pause.*) Why did you want to see me? Don't shake. You're safe here. (*Pours another drink.*) Where do you come from?

**Buddy**  Plaistow.

**Albert**  Whereabouts?

**Buddy**  Do you now the Greengate pub?

**Albert**  I've pissed a fortune down the Greengate's porcelain.

**Buddy**  Well down that road – near the docks.

**Albert**  Docks closed now.

**Buddy**  Yeah.

**Albert**  Have another. (*Drinks.*)

**Buddy**  Tar. Making me head spin.

**Albert**  Good. Biggest docks in the world, my day – the London docks. Seen as many as 85 vessels in the Royals. Queueing up to get in – all the way from Gallion's Reach to Tower Bridge. Passed there the other week. Three vessels I counted. Three.

**Buddy**  In our road, all the men worked there. Dockies.

**Albert**  Something special about a dockie. In the city, a man of the sea. Hard job.

**Buddy**  Tough blokes.

**Albert**  No dockies in Plaistow now.

**Buddy**  No docks.

**Albert**  On the run, are you?

*Pause.*

You can tell me . . .

**Buddy**  I did know a bloke once. Who was on the run. From Borstal.

**Albert**  Borstal eh? I know about those places. According to the Jay report more than 11,000 out of the 12,000 kids in Borstals shouldn't be there.

**Buddy**  Comedian, is he?

**Albert**  His father-in-law is. This Jay bloke is married to the Prime Minister's daughter.

**Buddy**  Makes them sound like the Marx brothers.

**Albert**  Listen Chubby chops, whatever you've done – it can't be that bad.

**Buddy**  Nar?

**Albert**  We all make mistakes.

**Buddy**  Have you?

**Albert**  I beg your pardon?

**Buddy**  Lord Plaistow.

**Albert**  Yerrs.

**Buddy**  Mistakes? You made?

**Albert**  Fill a Hansard.

**Buddy**  A what?

**Albert**  Where they report it all, every word you say in Parliament.

**Buddy**  Lord Plaistow. All grand this. All lush and smelling posh and rich things and – you called Lord Plaistow. You don't live in Plaistow. In the slums. Do you, Lord.

**Albert**  I did, once.

**Buddy**  Very honoured, you know. Very honoured you call yourself Lord Plaistow.

**Albert**  A tribute to my ex-constituents, when they moved me into the Upper House.

**Buddy**  Felt all honoured and flattered we did, down in the slums. I . . . I . . . (*Holds his face.*) Pain is going right into me head.

**Albert**  Your face . . . ?

**Buddy**  I got some stuff, for me tooth. Got any hot water, governor?

**Albert**  Water? I suppose there must be some here somewhere . . . (*Exits.*)

**Buddy**  Tooth on fire. Tooth is. Screaming in me head. Get this fixed and . . . everything'll be all right.

**Albert** *returns with a bowl.*

Won't it?

**Albert**  Poor kid . . . here, let me see.

**Buddy**  (*his face close to* **Albert**'s)   When you open your mouth, all I smell is brandy and see gold.

**Albert**  Still me own teeth.

**Buddy** Polish them with Brasso?

**Buddy** *fixes the temporary filling in his mouth.* **Albert** *smiles and strokes* **Buddy**'s *hair.*

**Albert** Skin so smooth. Shiny hair. And freckles around your nose. Not an ounce of spare flesh on you. (*Pause.*) You remind me about everything that was good about being young. Wide open eyes, no longer innocent. Where did you lose that, beautiful Cockney boy? With your red lips and your pale skin . . .

**Buddy** You bent? Are you?

**Albert** *pauses, then roars with laughter and tops up their two glasses.* **Buddy** *sets down the bowl and puts his feet up on the sofa, hands behind his head.*

**Albert** For God's sake, relax, boy, relax. It's . . . err . . . it's . . . oh yes, it's Christmas. Time for joy. Time for celebration. For festivity. Bit of . . . awash with happiness.

**Buddy** Happiness? After what I done?

**Albert** Shall I get you drunk, Chubby Chops?

**Buddy** Why should I care? Safe here. Warm and safe.

**Albert** Drink from the goblet. Drink it all down fast. Anaesthetise the pain of your tooth and your cares. Ah dentist! Dentist! The dinner party tonight – there'll be a dentist. Chubby, I shall take you to dinner. A feast.

**Buddy** Right what I fancy.

**Albert** But there'll be a dentist there. Woman, bit snobby, like she's got a champagne bottle permanently lodged up her arsehole – her husband's a dentist, he'll be there. We shall be on our way. If I can get a Minicab. This clobber, can't stand in the street hailing a cab. (*Laughs at* **Buddy** *and winks.*) They might think I'm a pouf.

**Albert** *dials on the phone and waits.* **Buddy** *bounces up and down on the sofa, laughing.*

**Buddy** I ain't stupid.

**Albert** Nar, you ain't.

**Buddy** All your friends be there, eh?

**Albert** Well, sort of. One does not have such a large spectrum of choice when one has . . . impaled the sanctity of one's party's image.

**Buddy**  Labour Party?

**Albert**  Nothing else.

**Buddy**  You don't know nothing about me.

**Albert**  Sammy sent you. That's a recommendation.

**Buddy**  Are you taking the piss out of me?

**Albert**  No.

**Buddy**  I'm pissed.

**Albert**  I'm pissed.

**Buddy**  Where are we going then?

**Albert**  A splendid dinner. Lose your terrors tonight.

**Buddy**  Are you pissing me about?

**Albert**  No. (*Pause.*) I want to kiss you . . .

**Buddy** *raises his arm and fist as though to strike* **Albert**. *Then he flips his wrist in an effeminate gesture and offers the back of his hand to be kissed.* **Albert** *gropes* **Buddy**'*s upper thigh and laughs.*

*Blackout. Football crowd roaring. Lights up on a urinal beneath the grandstand at West Ham football ground. Crowd noises continue off.* **Ronnie** *and* **Al** *urinate.*

**Ronnie**  I feel like I've been doing this all bloody night.

**Al**  Handy us sneaking in the last ten minutes. They open the gates early so the poor bleeders can get out and miss the punishment, eh. (*Laughs.*)

**Ronnie**  What we'll do is, we'll get behind the goal. There's bound to be someone there who we know. Alibis.

**Al**  Still losing 1-0. By God, they're going to be relegated this season – straight into the fourth division.

*They step away from urinal, zipping flies.*

**Ronnie**  Right, this is what we'll do. Are you listening to me Al?

**Al**  Was that a goal?

*They listen to the roar.*

**Ronnie**  Don't know. Now knock back some of this scotch. Get a real smelly breath. What we'll do is, soon as the match finishes we'll dash down onto the pitch and knock a copper's hat off, rough him up a bit. All Christmas piss-artist's like. Perfect alibi. Cop'll arrest us. If he's arrested us for hitting him, how could we have been doing the houses in Walnut Close, eh?

**Al** Brilliant Ronnie, brilliant. Your old lady, she's right. Brains like yours, you could have been Prime Minister.

**Ronnie** Dumped the heavy stuff, OK. But as soon as the heat's died off, we'll dig up the jewellery from the sandpit outside the flats, right? Thousands, thousands we've stacked down there.

**Al** Bastard little brother-in-law, you should have shot him.

**Ronnie** Yeah, well. All right now. Handed Pam a few sleepers so she'll be out of her head even if the Old Bill tries to give her the ol' M15.

**Al** So, we was here all night?

**Ronnie** From seven-thirty – here at the match.

**Al** Great alibi.

**Ronnie** Yeah. I got this one from a geezer in the Scrubs. A little variation, mind. He didn't do the job he was in for. Swears it, the robbery. I believed him. Classy bint, bit educated like, she took him to see some fucking Italian film. All foreign. Antonioni or something. Next day the law comes round his house about this job. He says: 'No, weren't me. I went to see this film. What was it called?' 'Can't remember', he says. 'What was it about?' they says. 'Good fucking question,' he says. 'I don't know.' Bint had pissed off. He got eighteen months.

**Al** That's why I never go to foreign films. Unless they're hard porn.

*Enter* **Sammy.**

**Sammy** Ronnie!

**Ronnie** Sammy, son. Sammy. Hello. Happy Christmas. Al here. Don't forget you saw us both here. Tonight.

**Sammy** I'm looking for someone bent.

**Al** Oi, watch it!

**Ronnie** Sammy listen, me and Al here – you saw us before the game started, didnt' you?

**Sammy** Anything you say, Ronnie. Anything you say.

**Ronnie** Good lad. (*Hands* **Sammy** *a fiver*)

**Sammy** Ronnie, that's very generous of you. But I've got something for you.

**Ronnie** (*laughs contemptuously*) Got to get down behind the goal, dad. Behind the goal.

**Sammy** But Ronnie, I've got some gear.

**Ronnie** Knocked off nylons? (*Laughs.*)

**Sammy** Just the sort of stuff you specialise in. I got some . . . sell it to you. Looking for a fence. But, old time's sake. I'll sell it to you.

**Al** Not tonight, grandad. Not tonight.

**Sammy** Always sell knocked off valuables in here – in the shit house.

**Ronnie** That's a bit where we are tonight, Sammy old son. So, look, piss off will you?

**Sammy** But Ronnie! Must be worth thousands and thousands. I only want a hundred or so. Necklaces and rings and watches and wonderful jewellery.

**Al** Got to get down –

**Sammy** Look. (*Produces a necklace from his raincoat pocket.*) See, real class, real classy.

**Ronnie** *inspects it.*

**Ronnie** Where did you get this?

**Sammy** Ask me no questions.

**Ronnie** I am asking you, dad. Where did you get this gear?

**Sammy** A contact. I can't say.

**Al** Ronnie . . . (*Looking at the necklace.*)

**Ronnie** (*grabbing* **Sammy***'s throat*) Sammy . . .?

**Sammy** Can't say Ronnie, can't say. Contact, contact. Big job. Can't reveal my sources. Just offering you a bargain.

**Ronnie** Can't reveal your sources? Who the bloody hell would hand you gear like this, you smelly, farting old windbag. I'll tell you where you got this gear, you child molesting old cunt. Out of the fucking sand-pit outside my flats. That's where you got it.

**Sammy** How do you know?

**Ronnie** 'Cause that's where I fucking buried it, you evil, stinking old bastard.

**Sammy** It's yours?

**Ronnie** Of course it's fucking mine. Al, stuff his head down the lavatory bowl, make him drown.

**Sammy** Ronnie, I'm sorry about this. I don't know what to say. Is it hot?

**Ronnie** Hot he says, hot! My God, it's fucking vindaloo. Put it this way. Two hours ago, this gear here – (*Shakes* **Sammy** *and discovers more jewellery in his coat.*) My God, how much more have you got here? Jesus Christ, not three hours ago this little lot was stinking of Bluebell Polish in safes all over Hornchurch.

**Sammy** I'm sorry, Ronnie. Sorry.

**Al** I'll drown his head in the piss-pot.

**Ronnie** Anyone see you lift it?

**Sammy** See me, see me?

**Ronnie** Digging up the sandpit?

**Sammy** No, no, honest. No-one. Except a kid.

**Ronnie** A kid?

**Sammy** Poor little bleeder. On the run, I think. From Borstal.

**Ronnie** Jesus Christ Almighty. I'm going to piss meself again. I'm going to have a heart attack before I set foot in Teneriffe. Give us, give us, give us.

*He removes all valuables from* **Sammy** *and puts them in his leather overcoat pockets.* **Al** *leads* **Sammy** *off. A door bangs and sound of screams and a lavatory cistern.* **Al** *returns, tugging down his sleeves.*

**Al** Well, we go and lay out the law then for the alibi?

**Ronnie** Al, I've got five grands worth of sparklers tickling under me armpits. He didn't find all of it, thank Christ.

**Al** More still there, good.

**Ronnie** Got a Rennie? For me heartburn.

**Al** Nar.

**Ronnie** We'd better get out of here.

**Al** Yeah.

**Ronnie** Dump this little lot of Sammy's somewhere.

**Al** The sandpit?

**Ronnie** Nar, somewhere less obvious. Somewhere more safe . . .
like –

**Al** Like?

**Ronnie** Somewhere where no-one would think of looking. Pam's
old mum.

**Al** What about her?

**Ronnie** Her old lady, she's in hospital, right?

**Al** Right.

**Ronnie** Stuff the jewellery on her. I mean, the old Bill'd never
think of looking for knocked off gear on some old cow dying in
hospital, right.

**Al** Nar. you're a genius Ronnie, a genius.

**Ronnie** Then, when the heat's died off, collect the gear off her.
Very safe deposit box, that old lady.

**Al** Ronnie, without you, I'd only be half the man I am without you.

**Ronnie** Let's shoot up the hospital.

*A great roar from crowd off.*

**Al** That a goal?

**Ronnie** Two goals in one match? This can't be West Ham . . .

*They run off as Blackout.*

*Lights up on* **Henry** *and* **Edna**'s *room.* **Henry** *leads on* **Albert.** **Henry**
*wears a party hat and apron; he is pouring wine.* **Albert** *wears his Santa
Claus suit and carries a sack of presents.* **Albert** *sits,* **Henry** *hands him a
glass.*

**Henry** Well? What do you think?

**Albert** Not a great vino man, Henry, not a vino man. I've never
been convinced those damned Froggies would go to all the trouble
of getting out of the vat when they're tramping the grapes to go for
a piss.

**Henry**  Albert, really! Aren't you going to behave yourself?

**Albert**  I thought the only reason you invited me was in the hope that I wouldn't.

**Henry**  R . . . r . . . really.

**Albert**  You really must do something about the infernal stutter Henry. You'll never get on *Call My Bluff.*

**Henry**  Patrick C . . . C . . . Campbell.

**Albert**  Mind you, the Liberals seem to hog it. I hear the last time there was a three line whip, the BBC had to cancel the show.

**Henry**  (*sipping wine*)  Mmm.

**Albert**  No spitting in the tram.

**Henry**  Pardon?

**Albert**  Old notice, on the trams and trolley-buses. No spitting. If you're going to gob, just gob, I say.

**Henry**  Fine bouquet.

**Albert**  Not a bad drop of plonk.

**Henry**  You're very honoured. Only five bottles left. On my 21st birthday, my father laid down two dozen bottles.

**Albert**  On my 21st birthday, my father laid the barmaid at the Princess Alice. Family scandal. He was a character. A drayman for the brewery. You and he . . . (*Pause.*) I don't think you two would have gotten on.

*Enter* **Edna** *with party hat.*

**Edna**  Albert darling! Here's your party hat.

**Albert**  Happy Christmas, Edna. Nice of you to ask me. I say, this is all jolly festive. Even Bubbles there looks happy.

**Henry**  I . . . I . . . I . . . (*He takes of his Pears Soap apron.*)

**Edna**  I must say you've been quiet lately, Albert. I miss reading about you in the *Evening Standard.*

**Albert**  They got off me back when Harold kicked me into the Lords. Into the ermine trust and stuffed a chamber pot on me barnet.

**Edna**  You always used to seem to be falling out of taxis and touching up the American ambassador and farting at Mrs Thatcher –

**Albert**   I know the Tories have been blown even further to the right lately but I can't claim full responsibility.

*He hands them wrapped presents from his sack.*

**Henry**   I say Albert, that's jolly kind of you. You shouldn't have gone to all this trouble.

**Albert**   They're left-overs from the Great Ormond Street party. I've no idea what they might be.

*They open the presents: an Actionman for* **Henry**, *a false beard and glasses for* **Edna**.

**Edna**   And for you Albert. (*Hands him a bottle of Chivas Regal. He has a party hat on now.*)

**Albert**   What's her name?

**Edna**   Who?

**Albert**   And her fellow – what do you call him?

**Edna**   Oh, Joan and Peter.

**Albert**   The kid, my young guest . . .

**Edna**   Where is he?

**Henry**   In the loo. Upset stomach.

**Albert**   And toothache. Got this damned toothache. Is the dentist bloke coming?

**Edna**   Yes, yes. Joan's collecting him from the station in the next half an hour.

**Albert**   Good. Have a look at the kid.

**Edna**   What's he like?

**Albert**   Seems . . . pretty ordinary. Some little problem or other, but he seems a bit shy about it.

**Edna**   We thought it would be so nice to share a real old fashioned Christmas. You do think it's a good idea, don't you Albert?

**Albert**   I wouldn't say no to another G and T.

**Henry**   You haven't had a G and T.

**Albert**  Then it's about bloody time I did. Large glass Henry.

**Edna**  I wrapped up a present for the child. One of Adam's favourite old toys. Do you suppose he is all right? He seems to have been up there an awfully long time.

**Albert**  My fault. I fear I plied him with a little too much hospitality. Forget how kids vomit on the booze . . .

**Buddy** *stands there.*

**Buddy**  Here I stand, broken hearted. Spent a penny and only farted.

*Pause.*

Funny shaped bog. I couldn't find the chain.

**Henry**  Ah, the bidet . . .

**Edna**  O. I had anticipated someone a little younger. O do come in, do. We're so delighted you accepted our invitation. Do sit down, do. Or just wander freely if you like. Whatever you'd prefer to do. Just treat the place like home, after all, you're our guest. Adam –

**Henry**  Our son –

**Edna**  He was just about your age, when he was younger.

**Henry**  My wife means –

**Edna**  Adam used to spend an awful lot of time just lying on the floor picking his toenails so I mean, really, you treat the place like home.

**Buddy** (*to* **Albert**, *who he sits beside*)  What's she going on about?

**Albert**  Let's all have a drink I say.

**Henry**  OK old chap. Good to meet you. Any friend of Lord Plaistow's is a friend of ours. Just relax, you know. We're all pretty relaxed and free and easy here. Just spend Christmas in the way we usually spend the f . . . f . . . festive season.

**Edna** (*sits beside* **Buddy**)  Adam would adore your safety pins.

**Buddy**  What?

**Edna**  Around your trousers.

**Buddy**  To hold them up.

**Edna**  Adam's got one in his nose.

**Buddy**  Must be fucking long trousers.

*Pause.*

**Henry**  I beg your pardon.

**Buddy**  If he clips his trousers up to his nose.

**Edna**  I mean – punk.

**Henry**  I meant your language. There are no house rules here, but I mean, after all, it is Christmas.

**Albert**  Behave lads. No cussing in front of the ladies. Edna here, she's a lady.

**Edna**  We've got a present for you.

**Buddy**  Eh?

**Edna**  A present for you.

**Buddy**  For me?

**Edna**  Yes.

**Buddy**  What did you get a present for me for?

**Edna**  Because it's Christmas.

**Buddy**  I ain't got nothing for you.

**Edna**  O, that doesn't matter. One doesn't give in the expectation of getting something in return. One gives simply for the pleasure of giving.

**Buddy**  I did have a duck, but I give it to me Auntie Connie.

**Henry**  I doubt she'll cook it as I'm cooking the duck tonight.

**Edna**  I didn't realise you had a family. I thought you'd be an orphan at least.

**Buddy**  Everyone's got a family.

**Edna**  Yes, but –

**Albert**  The old drinks seem to be getting a little cold, Henry. Old Chubby Chops here hasn't had one yet.

**Henry**  Ah yes, what would you like?

**Buddy**  Drunk a lot already. Lord Plaistow, he kept topping me up when I weren't looking. So he could have a grope in the cab.

**Albert** *laughs and gropes him.* **Henry** *pours* **Buddy** *a beer.*

**Edna** Open the present then. And a party hat, you're not wearing a party hat.

*She puts party hat on* **Buddy**'s *head while he opens the present. A meccano set.*

**Buddy** O, lovely. Right what I needed.

**Henry** Cheers.

**Edna** Happy Christmas

**Buddy** Ain't Christmas yet.

**Henry** Well, this is our Christmas. You see, we shall be away at Christmas.

**Edna** A fact-finding tour to the West Indies.

**Buddy** O.

**Edna** Your face looks terribly swollen.

**Buddy** Tooth hurting.

**Henry** Toothache can be ex . . . ex . . . ex . . .

**Edna** Excruciating.

**Henry** Extremely painful. Remember I had it at the by-election. What with the dashing about, it was days before I got it treated.

**Edna** I had toothache in Saudi Arabia one year.

**Albert** I've never been on one of those fag-finding trips.

**Henry** Albert really! (*Laughs.*)

**Albert** Not bugged, are we?

**Buddy** Me Auntie Connie . . .

*Pause*

**Albert** Your Auntie Connie?

**Buddy** This'll make you laugh. She had this bad tooth and she went to this dentist and he said: 'That's bad, got to come out.' Then he says 'Blimey, here's another one what ought to come out' and then 'Christ, here's another one that ought to be extracted' and he says to her 'It's your decision like, what do you reckon?' and me Auntie Connie, she says: 'Sod it, take them all

out' and when she come round after the gas, she never had a
tooth left in her head. He'd taken *all* her teeth out and she only
meant the three bad 'uns. What a laugh! She was right worried
about what Uncle Harold was going to say. 'Cause he always
reckoned she was bit of a daft old cow and she didn't much like
him thinking she was a nutter, stands to reason, so he was meeting
her outside the dentist's, like in the park and he had the Thermos
with him and some cheese and pickle rolls and he says to her:
'Got your favourites, crusty ones!'

*They all laugh.*

She threw up over him. (*Pause, he stands.*) This was before they
moved, into the country. Suffolk. Lovely there. The smell of the
hay burning in the fields. Country smells. Breathe in the good
country smells and you don't get in no more trouble, he said.
Smell the country in this room. And flowers. Roses at Christmas?

**Edna** (*shows him the roses in the bowl*) In October, the second
bloom. Every year I cut a dozen roses and put them in the deep
freeze and then thaw them just before Christmas. Yes, the roses
do smell beautiful.

**Buddy** Can even cut flowers and freeze them? Freeze the smell of
a rose? Breathe in the smell of the goodness and you won't get
into any more trouble, he said.

**Henry** I've rather lost you, I'm afraid.

**Buddy** O . . . Me Uncle Harold said . . . the country, good things,
London, he said, London – it's over.

**Henry** That could be Albert talking –

**Albert** I spent a lifetime speaking; street corners, outside the
dock gates, in the House. Words have no force, you know. To
change things. He's the man your Uncle should thank. He's in
the misgovernment.

**Henry** That kind of emotional Socialism is dead Albert.
Lansbury's dead, Nye's dead –

**Buddy** Marc Bolan's dead.

**Albert** Bloody Socialism's dead. Made extinct by his brand of
government by accountancy. And, God help us, East London's
dead.

**Henry** I agree I haven't held a seat there for quite as long as you

Albert, but –

**Albert** Dockland without the docks! Two decades ago, an impossibility.

**Henry** Newer industry, better housing. Anyway, the docks is only some emotional symbol. They were destined for the knackers' yard anyway in London, what with the larger vessels, containerisation –

**Albert** Bollocks.

**Edna** Albert, you mustn't swear wearing a party hat.

**Albert** Old Chubby Chops and me . . . (*Helps himself to another drink.*) We passed through what used to be the docklands in the Minicab. Took the road by the river, to here, Hornchurch. People down there, they're treated like driftwood. Places, didn't hardly recognise. Not a tinkle of a piano, not a throb of the old lifeblood. Memories bubbling about. I don't know whether it was the alcohol or flashes of genuine inspiration. Memories. New Year's Eves. Teeming with life. Childhood, adolescence, before the war, in the bitter winter afterwards. And every New Year's Eve, the ritual afterwards; just before midnight, we'd all take our glasses out into the backyard and see in the New Year. We'd stand out there in the dark and the frost, all the backyards full of neighbours. A hush. Looking towards the docks. The darkness pinpricked with coloured lights, along the funnels and the rigging of the vessels, outlining the cranes and running the lengths of the warehouse roofs. And at midnight, all the vessels from the seven oceans would sound their horns. Could hear them the entire length of the waterfront. Hundreds, hundreds. Giant, metallic choir. This year, there won't be a sound. Three vessels we counted, didn't we Chubby? Three vessels. God dammit, Hitler made the London docks his prime target at the height of the Blitz. Smash the London docks and you've smashed London. Night after night, we'd come out of the shelter; docks blazing, sky a brilliant carrot red. Kept the docks opens, kept England's artery pumping. Our own legislators know how to do it. Simple. Rubber stamp.

**Henry** O Albert. Times pass, things change.

**Albert** Nothing wrong in keeping the past as a lodestar.

**Henry** An uncle of mine, he did fire watching there you know. During the war. He says he'll never forget the night a German airman landed in the backyard of a pub. As though he'd just dropped in for a quick one. (*Laughs.*) They gave him a pint before they handed him over. He thought he was going to be lynched. His face. Docks blazing and – my uncle always says, his face – the hospitality. He says, that moment he knew we'd win the war.

**Albert** That's the difference between us Henry. My lot was out fighting Hitler's mob and your lot was buying them fucking drinks.

**Edna** You're both boring our little guest. Henry, the dinner –

**Henry** Ah.

**Albert** Everything's up to auction, to the highest bidder.

**Henry** Albert, you had the chance right after the war to create the ideal. Homes for heroes! New industries for a deprived area. You let the chance go begging –

**Edna** Now stop! You're boring our young friend.

**Buddy** I don't know what no-one's talking about.

**Henry** He's been bored to distraction by Albert's morbid memories. The good Lord Plaistow. Heavy booted man of the people.

**Albert** Until they kicked me upstairs and – into the ermine truss and stuck a chamber pot on me barnet.

**Henry** And avoided a scandal.

**Albert** O, if it's to avoid scandals, they'd better build an extension to the House of Lords and let out the Commons as a dormitory for Japanese tourists.

**Henry** O come, I think there are quite enough hotel rooms. I mean, you should know far better than I. You sat on the board of one of the property companies that did so much of the building work in the beloved homeland.

**Albert** I was defending the people I care for, safeguarding their interests.

**Henry** O, quite.

**Albert** My intention in accepting the directorship was to ensure that they constructed as many cubic feet of homes as hotel space, as yachting marinas.

**Henry**  Pretty bloody unsuccessfully.

**Albert**  I never understood what those city slickers were talking about.

**Henry**  You did very well of yourself out of the proceeds. Grand apartment in Westminster. *Ideal Home* magazine material.

**Albert**  Comfort for me old age. God dammit, I gave the best years of me life for peanuts.

**Henry**  You're just a hypocrite, Albert.

**Albert**  At least my intentions were honourable.

**Henry**  That's no defence.

**Albert**  And what about you Henry? What's this, your latest winter holiday jaunt? Jamaica again? Another fact-finding tour? Three winter holidays you've had there at the expense of the Jamaican government promising them you'll do a new deal to re-balance the sell-out for their sugar industry for the EEC. All of it is yet another free perk

**Edna**  I absolutely insist you two stop talking politics. It's so dreadfully boring. It's all argument and shouting. And the ridiculous truism is – you'll never alter each others opinions. It all depends on your point of view.

**Buddy**  Eh?

**Edna**  I said, it all depends on your point of view.

**Buddy**  See! That's it. What I want someone to do.

**Edna**  What?

**Buddy**  Like someone who's good at talking and arguing an' that. Like, that's why I come to you Lord Plaistow. 'Cause Sammy said you could help.

**Albert**  How?

**Buddy**  Explain to them. That it was an accident.

**Henry**  What was?

**Buddy**  What I done.

**Edna**  What do you mean?

**Buddy**  Like, well. The way you two were going at it like hammer and tongs, but you both reckon some of the things you done sounds a bit wrong if you don't get the chance to explain how it happened. (*Pause.*) Well, like, see . . . if you'd just explain to the governor . . . it was an accident.

**Henry** What was?

**Buddy** What I done.

**Edna** What do you mean?

**Buddy** This afternoon . . . how I spiked this screw. It weren't really a murder. I'm in a bit of a fix. And this fucking toothache. If I get this fixed, everything'll be all right, won't it . . .

*Pause, then Blackout.*

*Radio message from police.*

*Back projection of exterior hospital, night, deserted street. A Christmas tree lit up outside.*

*Spotlight on* **Pam**, *standing with a suitcase.*

**Pam** (*to audience*) They told me to bring her case of things. They phoned up. I thought they meant she was coming home, for Christmas. But I was a bit muddled with the Mogadons. When I eventually got here, she was gone. They'd transferred her. To Birmingham. For the blood. They'd rushed her up to Birmingham before I got the chance to get here. What a night, eh, what a night? When I heard the phone, I thought it was in a dream. It was so vivid. I thought the phone was ringing in Teneriffe. I've seen the brochures of the apartments. I showed them to mum. She said: 'Nice.' She was very taken. She could have come and stayed. Not in the summer, 'cause she don't like the heat, see. But in the winter, for a bit of winter sunshine. We would have had our Christmas dinner on the patio. I don't know about a roast, but something nice, not oily. Sitting on the patio looking out at the sea with the palm trees making shadows in the sunshine. With mum and Buddy. Buddy. And after dinner we'd have all gone down to the pool on this estate we had in mind in Teneriffe. You only have to pay £3 a month for full access; all the apartments' residents can use it, for £3 a month. The lady in the greengrocers told me. And I thought perhaps Buddy could get a job out there, on the estate. Away from all the bad influences. Know what I mean? And I was swimming and I got out of the pool and mum was sitting there under a sunshade at a table beside the pool and she was knitting this little white baby suit and I said: 'Mum, what are you making?' and she just smiled and I knew,

knew it was for me baby. (*Pause.*) That's why I didn't hear the
door. I was so asleep. The Old Bill, they just smashed it down and
come in and took away all the stuff. All the teles and the coats and
the stereos and . . . everything. When they find Ronnie! That's it,
as far as I'm concerned. And when they find Buddy . . . When they
find him . . .

*Enter* **Ronnie** *and* **Al**.

**Ronnie**  Pam.

**Pam**  What are you doing here?

**Ronnie**  At the flats, nosey old cow next door, she said you'd shot
down to the hospital here.

**Pam**  I brought mum's things. I thought she was coming home for
Christmas.

**Ronnie**  Coming home?

**Pam**  No.

**Al**  I hate the smell of hospitals. Makes me feel ill.

**Ronnie**  Listen Pam, so Old Bill cleared out all the gear then?

**Pam** *begins to cry*.

**Al**  Ronnie, she's crying.

**Ronnie**  Hang about, hang about. For Christ's sake, Pam. This is
important.

**Pam**  Ronnie, I don't know why I don't hate you.

**Ronnie**  Pam, don't get sentimental.

**Pam**  You're a bastard, a right bastard.

**Al**  Ronnie, do you reckon she's all right?

**Ronnie**  Listen, Pam. A couple of hours ago we unloaded a few
grands worth of sparklers on your mum.

**Pam**  They've transferred her, to the Birmingham blood centre.

**Ronnie**  Fantastic ruby necklace, must be worth five grand. And
rings and –

**Pam**  I think she must be worse.

**Al**  Who must be?

**Pam**  Me mum.

**Ronnie**  Sorry about that.

**Pam**  It's the shame you've brought on the family. That's what's made her worse.

**Ronnie**  Don't say that. You don't know what you're talking about. She's a bit upset.

**Al**  She looks a bit upset.

**Pam**  I am upset. She's been transferred.

**Ronnie**  When?

**Pam**  Just before I got here. I brought her case and –

**Ronnie**  Jesus Christ! She looked as right as rain a couple of hours ago when I stuffed her the jewellery. She said it was the nicest Christmas present she'd ever had.

**Pam**  It was seeing you that made her relapse.

**Ronnie**  Listen Pam, you'd better have a word with the matron. See if they took the stuff off her before the transfer.

**Al**  (*slowly realising*)   If they've transferred her to Birmingham . . . say she's still got the jewellery?

**Ronnie**  Al, will you excuse us a moment. I must comfort my wife in her moment of distress.

**Al**  Eh?

**Ronnie**  Fuck off.

**Al**  O. I'll be outside.

*Al exits. Pause.*

**Ronnie**  Pam, I want you to go and see the matron. They might have taken the sparklers off her and bungled them in a safe or . . . Pam, I'm doing the decent thing. I'm telling you that Al and me are going to piss off for a bit, till the heat dies off. We need them jewels now to pay for the hideout.

**Pam**  Serves you right. It's all over Ronnie. I don't want this life no more. You've contaminated me. Like you've contaminated Buddy, poor Buddy. I've had enough of being married to a villain.

**Ronnie**  Sure, sure – but just this last favour.

**Pam** No.

**Ronnie** Pam.

*She spits in his face. He hits her. Pause.*

**Ronnie** Sorry love, I didn't mean, I . . .

*She holds her eye.* **Al** *enters.*

**Al** She all right?

**Ronnie** Bitch, stupid fucking bitch. Let's get to that fucking sand-pit.

**Ronnie** *and* **Al** *exit. Blackout. Police message.*

*Harsh dentist surgery lights up on* **Albert** *with a bottle and still in his Santa Claus clothes and* **Henry**, *in a fur overcoat.* **Buddy** *is half asleep in the dentist's chair.*

**Albert** Well?

**Henry** He's on his way.

**Albert** About time.

**Henry** If word of this leaks out . . . it doesn't bear thinking about.

**Albert** Doesn't bear thinking about.

**Albert** Doesn't it?

**Henry** I had to give Edna a tranquilliser. The press are going to love this, aren't they. 'Government Minister entertains on the run murderer to Christmas dinner.'

**Albert** In times of crisis, remember what Churchill said.

**Henry** What?

**Albert** I don't mind if I do. (*Takes a hefty swig from the bottle.*)

**Buddy** *groans, his eyes still closed.*

**Albert** God, get a move on Peter, get a move on. (*To* **Buddy**.) You'll be all right, lad. Dentist on his way. He'll send you to sleep.

**Henry** Yes, Albert'll recite you one of his speeches.

**Albert** The dentist'll know what to do. Treat you. You stuck a frozen eel up her nose. Have you phoned the police Henry.

**Henry** Not ex . . ex . . . exactly. My intention is to. But I was just p . . . p . . . pondering on what might be the best way of going about it.

**Albert** How do you mean?

**Henry** You see, we're both somewhat compromised. I mean, if the press get hold of this! Just see the headlines. 'Minister entertains . . .' It doesn't bear thinking about.

**Albert** I hadn't thought of that.

**Henry** Then it's about fucking time you did. Look, what I propose is . . . we anaesthetise what's his name here, treat him, and whilst he's comatose, transport him back to your flat, and then you telephone the police and tell them he's been in your flat all the time.

**Albert** And mysteriously had a tooth extracted.

**Henry** No. You phoned Peter and Peter went to your flat and did it. Code of ethics. He couldn't refuse to treat someone in pain.

**Albert** Now wait a minute. So when the shit hits the fan, it goes straight into my face?

**Henry** But Albert, you've had so little publicity lately. People will begin to think you're dead. You're infamous – I mean, legendary for helping kids in trouble.

**Albert** Don't be stupid. The kid'll tell them right away he was at your house.

**Henry** No, he was delirious with pain. And the story'll do wonders for your memoirs. Newspaper serialisations be worth a few thousand pounds. It can only benefit you.

**Albert** You may be right Henry. If I say –

**Buddy** Oi! You fucking bastards.

**Albert** OK Chubby, let's calm down –

**Buddy** Don't you talk to me, you pouffy bastard. Heard you. Heard you. Your plans. To get out. Get out of the embarrassment. That I caused you lot.

**Albert** Not me.

**Buddy** Going to make money out of me. Sell the story to the papers. You get rich out of what I done. I spent all night. I was so frightened. You ever been so frightened you think you're going to die? Die of fright? Talked to people, heard stories . . . legends . . . old fighter . . . villains . . . priest cheated me . . . All I wanted all the time was the chance to . . . explain . . . hospital, me mum dying . . .

her life . . . nothing – seen other lives, rich lives –

**Albert**  I slaved a lifetime to make more lives better.

**Buddy**  Ain't done much fucking good have you. All the kids inside, I mean . . . kids where I just come from, what they done seems a bit fucking pathetic compared to what you posh lot have done. Snotty drawers and her car fiddle. Only it's legal. But your Jamaican trip, that ain't is it Henry.

**Henry**  Perfectly acceptable practice.

**Buddy**  Come off it.

**Albert**  Actually, it's quite above board.

**Buddy**  What about your property company director lark?

**Albert**  Not illegal, not illegal.

**Buddy**  It must be.

**Albert**  No.

**Buddy**  Can't be right.

**Albert**  Absolutely right.

**Buddy**  Making money out of me?

**Albert**  I haven't done anything of the sort –

**Buddy**  Yet. You will. Your riches, all comes from other peoples' pain.

*Enter* **Joan** *in a fur coat.*

**Albert**  I thought you'd gone to get Peter

**Joan**  I'm not helping that vicious little shit. As far as I'm concerned, the police can chop off his bollocks with a rusty fret-saw.

**Henry**  Joan –

**Joan**  His photo's in the *Evening Standard*. Nationwide manhunt. Hanging's too good for the likes of him. And he stole £500 from my purse.

**Buddy**  Five hundred? (*Laughs, slurps.*)

**Joan**  Have you called the police?

**Henry**  We were just discussing the right approach.

**Joan**  There's only one. Pick up the phone and dial.

**Peter** *enters. In a white dentist's coat.*

**Albert**  Ah, there you are Peter –

**Henry**  Peter, perhaps you could restrain your wife before we've had the chance to –

**Peter** (*to* **Buddy**)  Open your mouth let's have a look.

*Takes the dentistry mirror and a tool from the table of instruments beside the chair.*

**Joan**  Use an axe.

**Henry**  You understand, our problem is basically that –

**Peter**  Please get out of my surgery.

**Henry**  But we must decide –

**Joan**  I shall call the murder squad.

**Peter**  Will you please leave my surgery and do your decision making some other place.

**Joan**  He's a murderer!

**Peter**  I'm a dentist. Go on, please.

**Albert**, **Henry** *and* **Joan** *exit.*

**Peter** *examines* **Buddy**'s *open mouth.*

**Peter**  Ah, I see . . .

*He takes the tweezers and removes a small temporary filling from a tooth cavity.*

This wasn't much good.

**Buddy**  I put it in. To try and stop it hurting. It still hurt though.

**Peter**  Now let's see. See what the trouble is. Cavity. Filling came out, a deep one and . . . this'll hurt.

**Buddy** *yells.* **Peter** *removes a tiny piece of silver paper from* **Buddy**'s *tooth.*

Silver paper. Chocolate on it. You should take the foil off before you eat it. Caught in the cavity.

**Buddy**  The village poufs. They brought in some chocolate before the match for us. We don't get it much.

**Peter**  What match?

**Buddy**  Football match. Prestige match with the village.

**Peter**  Tried to bribe you, did they?

**Buddy**  Eh?

**Peter**  To lose the game?

**Buddy**  O. It don't hurt now.

**Peter**  Silver paper touching the nerve. Bet it did hurt. Needs a new filling.

**Buddy**  Another time. Just wanted the pain to stop. Clear me head of the pain. Clearer now. Thank you.

**Peter**  What?

**Buddy**  For helping me.

**Peter**  It's my job.

**Buddy**  Know what I done?

**Peter**  Yes, I heard.

**Buddy**  Don't you . . . hate me?

**Peter**  Hate you?

**Buddy**  Everyone, when they saw me, heard what I done. They went berserk. Like I was the plague or something.

**Peter**  Well, some people, they over-react.

**Buddy**  You remind me of the priest. So calm. So . . . calm. So peaceful. Relaxing. Then he betrayed me, sounded the alarm.

**Peter**  I suppose he thought he was doing what he should do.

**Buddy**  Bit generous, aren't you?

**Peter**  Why not be? There's enough who aren't.

**Buddy**  I don't understand you. I gave your missus the shits.

**Peter**  Yes. (*Brief laugh.*) She told me.

**Buddy**  Don't you want revenge? To punish me like?

**Peter**  I think there's enough who want to punish. I don't feel any inherent need to . . . pay-back.

**Buddy**  You're kind.

**Peter** Kind?

**Buddy** The screw, he was kind.

**Peter** Are you going to stab me?

**Buddy** (*takes a syringe from the table*) I could – with this needle.

**Peter** Maybe.

**Buddy** Aren't you frightened?

**Peter** I don't think you want to stab anyone.

**Buddy** I didn't want to make him die.

**Peter** Accident?

**Buddy** Accident, yeah.

**Peter** Would you like someone to speak for you? Perhaps I could help you . . . explain. To them. To the governor.

**Buddy** Who?

**Peter** Me.

*Silence.*

**Buddy** (*giggles*) All night . . . all night . . . I've been looking . . . looking for someone to do that.

**Peter** Well?

**Buddy** Bit late now. Too late. Now it's too late.

**Peter** It's never too late.

**Buddy** The time has passed when it could work.,

**Peter** Well. You can't run away for ever.

**Buddy** So?

**Peter** I'll have to tell them.

**Buddy** Yeah?

**Peter** It's my duty. To phone the police.

**Buddy** I could do a bunk, out the fire exit there . . . while you're on the phone.

**Peter** You said it yourself. Every hour's delay in going back makes it worse. I shall phone the police now.

**Peter** *exits.* **Buddy** *takes the screw's whistle from his pocket and fingers it as the lights begin to fade. Enormous back projection of the empty docks at night. One vessel amid the cranes. A ship's horn sounds. The snow begins to fall.*

*Darkness, just the back projection.*

*Lights up, still snowing.*

*The sandpit snow-covered and the tractor tyre swing.*

*Another foghorn sounds as* **Ronnie** *and* **Al** *enter hurriedly with torches and two leather grips. They go to the sandpit.*

**Ronnie**  Right, here we go, then catch that plane.

**Al**  Have to get our skates on. Should have gone to Birmingham first and got the jewels off the old cow. What a waste.

**Ronnie**  Enough here. Let's dig it up.

**Al**  I've never been to Teneriffe Ronnie.

**Ronnie**  Good old Frank. There's a real mate. Time of crisis, one phone call and he's got us two airline tickets. Class. No Panic Frank. Flights on the first plane. Just get up the rest of this gear and, away.

**Al**  Six thousand pounds.

**Ronnie**  Easy. I phoned Larry the Elbows. He's got the readies to buy the gear. Very organised, salvage job but –

**Al**  Very organised.

**Ronnie**  You have to be nowadays. No more coshing milkman. Bit of class. There'll be a lot redevelopment here now they've closed the docks. Posh area, it'll be. Make a fortune we shall. There's a lot of fucking money about.

**Al**  I just hope no-one's looking.

**Ronnie**  Relax Al. For Christ's sake relax. It's snowing. Foggy. No-one up there in the flats'll be able to see us.

**Al**  It's cold enough to freeze your bollocks off tonight. I'll keep a look out.

*He goes to flash the torch off.*

**Ronnie**  Three paces from the edge . . . (*Measures the spot in the sandpit.*)

**Al**  I'm freezing to death.

**Ronnie**  This time tomorrow you'll be sunbathing.

**Al**  Hey!

**Pam** *enters. She has a black eye.* **Al** *shines the torch on her face.*

**Pam**  It's only me.

**Ronnie**  What the bloody hell you doing here? I told you to piss off you cow. I never want to see you again in all my life.

**Pam**  I know. You told me when you split my eyeball.

**Ronnie**  Lost me temper.

**Pam**  You always have been impetuous.

**Ronnie**  Clear off, will you.

**Pam**  Frank rang, Frank from Heathrow. He said it's snowing.

**Ronnie**  I know it's fucking snowing.

**Al**  I know it's snowing.

**Pam**  He said the flight's been cancelled. The flight to Teneriffe, because of the snow. I never knew you was doing a bunk to Teneriffe. Ronnie, that news hurt me more than when you hit me. That was our dream. Ours.

**Ronnie**  Yeah, well. That's the way it goes.

**Pam**  Anyway, the flight's cancelled. You can't go tonight. I just thought I'd tell you. To save you a wasted journey.

**Al**  Fuck it.

**Pam**  I'll miss you Ronnie, in a funny way. Thing's will seem boring without you. Without a villain. Nice and better but . . . a bit boring.

*She goes.* **Al** *and* **Ronnie** *stare at each other.*

**Al**  What'll we do then?

**Ronnie**  Christ. Bloody women.

**Al**  That's why I never got married, Ronnie. Never settled down. Me mum put me off the idea.

**Ronnie**  What'll we do? Go to Heathrow. In the nice bar. Till there is a flight. Heathrow, here we come.

**Al**  Yeah.

**Ronnie**  Fucking Ada. I don't believe it.

**Al**  Get a move on Ronnie, I'm getting nervous.

**Ronnie**  Jesus, the bastard. The bastard. It's all frozen. It's all frozen over, like an ice rink.

**Al**  What are you talking about Ronnie?

**Ronnie**  All this fucking sleet, the cold. It's settled on the sandpit and frozen over. It's all frozen.

**Al**  But Ronnie – all the sparklers we nicked are buried under there.

**Ronnie**  Now tell me something I don't know.

**Al**  Mind you don't piss your pants again Ronnie.

**Ronnie**  Got a Rennie? Heartburn.

**Al**  Here. (*Hands him a packet.*) Got them from the nurses in the hospital.

**Ronnie**  Jesus.

**Al**  Crack open the ice. With a . . . with a . . . If only I hadn't dumped that fucking iron bar.

**Ronnie**  Need a pick axe or a . . .

**Al**  I ain't got a pick axe handy. Jump on it, smash it. Must smash the ice.

**Al** *and* **Ronnie** *jump up and down on the ice. They jump wildly, screaming. Then they tire. They stand breathing heavily.*

**Buddy** *has entered. He wears a long black leather overcoat. He watches them, grinning.*

**Buddy**  Pathetic.

**Ronnie** *is embarrassed by* **Buddy**'s *presence. He turns his back on* **Buddy.**

**Al**  Thousands under here.

**Ronnie**  It's fucked, it's a blow out, we've had it. The best night's work I've ever done. Let's find Bert and Ginger Jug Ears and find a card school. Come back and get it tomorrow.

**Al**  It'll have melted tomorrow.

**Ronnie**  Fucking better have.

*They exit hurriedly.* **Buddy** *laughs.*

*Sound of* **Sammy** *approaching singing* 'Goodbyee'. **Sammy** *enters, then suddenly aware of* **Buddy** *in the shadows.*

**Sammy**  Go on mug me, whoever you are. Mug me up. Kill me.

*He turns to see* **Buddy** .

**Sammy**  I took it, but they took it back.

**Buddy**  There's more buried down there. But it's all frozen over. They can't get at it.

**Sammy**  There's more? I never found it all? (*Laughs.*) You look like Ronnie.

**Buddy**  Ronnie? He's small time.

**Sammy**  The coat –

**Buddy**  Nicked it from a motor.

*Pause. Fog horn from docks.*

**Sammy**  What'll you do boy? You can't run away for ever. Once the docks was the place runaways went. Biggest docks in the world at one time. Miles and miles of ships. To far-away places. Stowaway on a ship. Hardly see a ship there now. There's one this tonight. It's all over here. London, East London – it's smashed. You and me, we're the casualties of the peace. There was a time they respected an honest fighting man. Time was they respected a villain. All that's gone.

**Buddy**  Docks gone. Houses gone. Can't kill the people.

**Sammy**  They've had a bloody good try.

**Buddy**  Take away the night you won your title?

**Sammy**  Never take away the night I won me title.

**Buddy**  Once a fighter?

**Sammy**  Always a fighter.

**Buddy**  Keep fighting?

**Sammy**  Keep fighting.

**Buddy**  What with?

**Sammy**  Need money?

**Buddy**  I give mine to you.

**Sammy**  I'll give you better than money boy (*Takes a necklace from his pocket.*) Ronnie never got this. I had it down me pants keeping me balls warm. Here, take it.

**Buddy**  What's the use of this to me, what I've done?

**Sammy**  Flog it. Face, swelling's gone down.

**Buddy**  Dentist fixed it. One of Lord Plaistow's friends.

**Sammy**  He helped?

**Buddy**  He's a villain.

**Sammy**  He is.

**Buddy**  Yeah, he's a villain.

*Another fog horn from a ship.*

**Sammy**  Getting ready to sail. Saw it, a Brazilian vessel. She'll never come back to the London docks.

**Buddy**  I used to lay in bed on foggy nights, listening to the sound of the horns. Wondering where they was going to. Rio de Janeiro and Marseilles and Australia and New York and . . . How do you stowaway on a vessel then?

**Sammy**  Easy. You walk on and then you hide. Like you've been doing ashore all night.

**Buddy**  Yeah.

**Sammy**  Need money for the bus – to get to the ship?

**Buddy**  I nicked a Government Minister's motor.

**Sammy**  Drive it in the river. They'll give him another one. Backhander.

**Buddy**  Keep fighting?

**Sammy**  You ain't evil, boy. I know you ain't evil.

**Buddy**  What I done ain't nothing compared to what a lot of people I met have done.

**Sammy**  I killed a man once, in the ring.

**Buddy**  Lord Plaistow, he telled me.

**Sammy**  Accident, scar for life.

**Buddy**  Mine an accident and all.

**Sammy**  Enough scars here. Desolation, all around. Want this? Be a tamed pigeon, boy? Never, not you, not me – we're fighters.

**Buddy**  Stowaway? On the ship?

**Sammy**  Take the necklace.

**Buddy**  Man died under a frozen stream. His last message – 'Goodbye cruel world.'

**Sammy**  There's another message. 'Fuck you cruel world.' I'd be an anarchist, but I can't spell it.

*Another horn.*

**Sammy**  If you're going to go . . .

**Buddy**  Yeah.

**Sammy**  Go boy go.

**Buddy**  If you see Pam –

**Sammy**  Pam?

**Buddy**  Ronnie's wife –

**Sammy**  Ah?

**Buddy**  Tell her, don't keep getting drunk.

**Sammy**  Like me?

**Buddy**  *hesitates, then goes.* **Sammy** *sits on the swing.*

**Sammy**  In court one day I was . . . it was me anniversary, me hundredth appearance for being drunk and disorderly. The magistrate, an intelligent man, deeply intelligent – do-gooder – he said he'd give me one last chance. Said he wouldn't put me in the cells. Stupid bastard. He said drink was my problem. Brilliant man. He said if I promised never to drink again, if I kept off the booze, he said he'd let me off. He said I mustn't touch a drop, not a drop. Not, he said, not even a glass of sherry before dinner.

*He laughs, swings, drinks from a bottle*

Be optimistic he said. Optimist. I sat on park swings in the twenties, thirties, in the depression. I saw bare-footed kids running wild in the streets with rickets in their legs and scars of malnutrition. You ever wondered why the East End threw up so many light weights and fly weights? Skinny kids without an ounce of spare flesh. I see them. I see them in the slums and I say: I've seen deprivation and poverty and seen rats chewing babies in slum rooms. But I ain't a pessimist. Smash down the manor, rip it up, smash it down, fuck up decent peoples' lives but – the tribe lives on. Kid there. Never give in, never surrender. Do what the fuck you like to us mister. Can't destroy that heart. It's in the blood. Never kill that. Never. Bon voyage kiddo, bon voyage.

*Horn sounds. Blackout.*

*Music loud. Boomtown Rats* 'Joey's on the Street Again' *from the album* Boomtown Rats, *Ensign label.*

*Titles in the*
*Methuen Modern Plays series*
*are listed overleaf.*

| | |
|---|---|
| Jean Anouilh | *Antigone* |
| | *Becket* |
| | *The Lark* |
| | *Ring Round the Moon* |
| John Arden | *Serjeant Musgrave's Dance* |
| | *The Workhouse Donkey* |
| | *Armstrong's Last Goodnight* |
| | *Pearl* |
| John Arden and | *The Royal Pardon* |
| Margaretta D'Arcy | *The Hero Rises Up* |
| | *The Island of the Mighty* |
| | *Vandaleur's Folly* |
| Wolfgang Bauer | *Shakespeare the Sadist* |
| Rainer Werner | |
| Fassbinder | *Bremen Coffee* |
| Peter Handke | *My Foot My Tutor* |
| Franz Xaver Kroetz | *Stallerhof* |
| Brendan Behan | *The Quare Fellow* |
| | *The Hostage* |
| | *Richard's Cork Leg* |
| Edward Bond | *A-A-America!* and *Stone* |
| | *Saved* |
| | *Narrow Road to the Deep North* |
| | *The Pope's Wedding* |
| | *Lear* |
| | *The Sea* |
| | *Bingo* |
| | *The Fool* and *We Come to the River* |
| | *Theatre Poems and Songs* |
| | *The Bundle* |
| | *The Woman* |
| | *The Worlds* with *The Activists Papers* |
| | *Restoration* and *The Cat* |
| | *Summer* and *Fables* |
| Bertolt Brecht | *Mother Courage and Her Children* |
| | *The Caucasian Chalk Circle* |
| | *The Good Person of Szechwan* |
| | *The Life of Galileo* |
| | *The Threepenny Opera* |
| | *Saint Joan of the Stockyards* |
| | *The Resistible Rise of Arturo Ui* |
| | *The Mother* |
| | *Mr Puntila and His Man Matti* |